MW01273008

ISBN: 9781290822022

Published by:
HardPress Publishing
8345 NW 66TH ST #2561
MIAMI FL 33166-2626

Email: info@hardpress.net
Web: http://www.hardpress.net

.

ON LIFE

Free Age Press.

ON LIFE.

BY LEO TOLSTOY

A New Translation by Mabel and Agnes Cook, based on the French Version of the Countess Tolstoy and MM. Tastevin. Carefully verified by and conformed to the unabridged Russian, chiefly by F. B. R Edited by A. C. Fifield.

NEW EDITION.

FREE AGE PRESS, Christchurch, Hants.
EVERETT & Co., 42, Essex Street, Strand, London.

CONTENTS

CONTENTS

CONTENTS

" Man is only a reed, the weakest in nature, but a thinking reed. It is not necessary that the universe in its entirety should arm itself to crush him. A vapour, a drop of water, is sufficient to slay him. But even were the universe to crush him, man would still be nobler than that which kills him, because he knows he dies. Of the advantage which the universe has over man it is unconscious. Thus the whole of our nobility consists in thought, and it is this which should elevate us, not space and time. Let us therefore strive to think well. Here is the principle of morality."

PASCAL.

" Two things fill the soul with always renewed and increasing wondering admiration the oftener and more deeply our thought is occupied with them : the starry sky above me and the moral law within me. . . . The first begins from the position which I occupy in the external world, and enlarges the connection in which I stand into superlative greatness, with its worlds upon worlds and systems of systems, and besides also into the limitless times of its periodical movements, of its beginnings and its durations.

" The second begins from my invisible self, from my personality, and exhibits me as in a world possessing the real endlessness, but which can be realised only by the reason and through which I realise myself, not, as in the first instance, only in an accidental connection, but in a complete and necessary connection."

KANT (Kritik of Practical Reason).

" A new commandment I give you : that ye love one another."

JOHN xiii. 34.

ON LIFE

INTRODUCTION

LET us suppose that a man has no other means of livelihood than a mill. The son and grandson of a miller, this man understands thoroughly, by tradition, how to manage all the parts of his mill so that it may work well. He knows nothing of mechanics, but he has adjusted all the mechanism as well as he can, so that the grinding may be effective and good—and thus the man lives and is fed.

But one day this man begins to reflect on the construction of his mill, and as he has now picked up some vague notions of mechanics he sets himself to observe what turns what.

Going from the mill-hoppers to the mill-stones, from the stones to the cylinder, from the cylinder to the wheels, then to the sluice, to the dam, to the river, he eventually comes to the conclusion that it all depends on the dam and the river. He is so happy in his discovery that instead of being anxious, as usual, about the quality of the flour, the raising and lowering of the mill-stones, the stretching and the slackening of the strap, he sets himself to study the river ; and his mill gets entirely out of order. People tell him that this is not the way to do work. He disputes this, and goes on reasoning about the river.

He examines so deeply and for so long a time this question, he discusses it so passionately with those who show him the falsity of his reasoning, that he ends by believing that the river is the mill.

To all the proofs which are given him of the falsity of his reasoning, the miller replies, " No mill can grind without water, therefore it is necessary, in order to understand the mill, to know how to let the water run ; to know the force of its current ; to know whence it comes : in a word, to understand the mill it is necessary to understand the river."

From the point of view of logic, the reasoning of the miller appears irrefutable. The only way to un-deceive him, is to show him that what is most important in all reasoning, is not so much the reasoning itself as the position which it occupies ; and that, to think with advantage, it is indispensable to know of what one must think in the first place, and what should be the results. It is necessary to show him that a rational activity is distinguished from an irrational activity merely by its arguments being arranged in order of importance. Such an argument should come in the first place, such other in the second place, in the third place, in the tenth place, and thus in order ; whilst an irrational activity arranges its arguments without connection. It is necessary to prove to him also that the establishment of that connection is not fortuitous, but that it depends on the end to which all the arguments are tending.

It is the end of all the reasoning which fixes the order in which the particular arguments should be arranged to be rational.

Every argument out of touch with the common end of all the reasoning is absurd, however logical it is in itself.

The aim of the miller is to grind well, and that end, if he does not lose sight of it, determines the order in which the reasonings upon the mill-stones, the wheels, the dam, and the river should be arranged.

Without that adaptation to the final aim, the reasonings of the miller, however logical and eloquent they may be in themselves, are false and, above all, useless; they are like the speculations of Kyfa Makëitch, the famous character of Gogol, who calculated what size the egg of an elephant would be, if elephants laid eggs like birds. Such are, in my opinion, the reasonings of contemporary science upon life.

Life is the mill which man wishes to study. The mill is necessary only in order to grind well; life is only necessary in order to be good. Man cannot with impunity lose sight for a single instant of this aim of his researches. If he does, his arguments will inevitably lose their right order, and be like those of Kyfa Makëitch when he calculated the quantity of gunpowder required to blow up the egg of an elephant.

Man only studies life in order to ameliorate it. It was thus that the men studied it who have advanced humanity in the path of knowledge. But, by the side of these true teachers, of these benefactors of humanity, there have always been, and there are now, reasoners who lose sight of the aim of the discussion and set themselves to find out the origin of life, why the mill turns. Some say it is because of the water, others because of the mechanism. The discussion grows heated, they get farther and farther away from the real object of the discussion, and finally end by substituting something entirely foreign to the original matter they discussed.

There is an old story about a discussion between a Jew and a Christian on faith. It is related that the Christian instead of replying to the subtilties of the Jew, gave him a smack on his bald head, and

asked him, "Which made the noise? Your bald
head or the palm of my hand?" and for the discussion upon faith was substituted a new question
impossible to determine. Something analogous to
this has existed from the earliest times, side by side
with the true wisdom of men regarding the question
of life.

Discussions on the origin of life date from a very
remote period. From what does it proceed? From
an immaterial principle or from the different com-
binations of matter? These discussions still continue,
and one cannot foresee the end, simply because the
aim of the discussion has been left on one side,
and life is discussed, regarded, independently of
its aim. By the word life one no longer understands
life itself but its origin, and the accompanying
phenomena.

At present, not only in scientific works, but in
conversation, when one speaks of life it is no longer
a matter of something we all know, of the life I am
conscious of through the sufferings I fear and hate,
and through the pleasures and joys which I desire,—
but rather a matter of something arising either by
chance, following certain physical laws, or else
arising from some cause which is a mystery.

To-day the word "life" is applied to something
debatable, which lacks the essential characteristics
of life, that is to say the sensations of suffering and
enjoyment and the aspirations towards good.

"Life is the sum of the functions which resist
death." "Life is the sum of the phenomena which
succeed each other during a limited time in an
organised being." "Life is a double process of
decomposition and combination, universal and
without interruption." "Life is a certain combination of modifications of various nature, which are
successively accomplished." "Life is the organism
in activity." "Life is a special activity of organic

matter." "Life is the adaptation of internal conditions to external conditions."

Without speaking of the errors and the tautologies
of which all these definitions are full, their essence
is always the same : they do not define what all men
equally comprehend under the name of life, but
certain processes which accompany life and other
phenomena.

Nearly all these definitions could be applied to
the activity of the crystal in formation ; some of
them to fermentation, to decay ; and all would be
suitable to the life of each cell in my body, for
which good and evil do not exist.

Certain processes which are accomplished in
crystals, in protoplasm, in the nucleus of protoplasm,
in the cells of our bodies and of other bodies, are
comprehended under the name of life ; whilst to us
that name is indissolubly connected with the consciousness of the aspiration towards well-being.

To reason upon certain conditions of life, taken
for life itself, is the same thing as to speak of the
river as if it were the mill. These arguments might
be very necessary for some purposes, but they do not
touch the object which they are intended to discuss,
and consequently all the conclusions about life drawn
from such reasoning cannot but be false.

The word "life" is short and very clear, and
everyone knows what it signifies. It is just because
everyone knows the meaning of it that we ought
always to employ it in the sense admitted by all.
The sense of this word is clear for everyone, not
because it is defined with precision by other words
or by other ideas, but on the contrary because it
expresses a fundamental idea whence flow many if
not all other ideas. Consequently, to draw deductions from that idea, we ought to accept it in its
central and indisputable meaning. And it is this
which is lost sight of, as it seems to me, in the

different discussions on the meaning of life. The result is that the fundamental idea of life, not having been taken in its central signification from the first, and having been drawn farther and farther away, in consequence of these controversies, from its essential and universally admitted meaning, has ended by entirely losing its primary signification and taking another which does not correspond with it. What has happened is this, that the centre from which the circles are drawn has been displaced and transferred to another point.

They dispute over whether life resides in the cell or in the protoplasm, or lower yet, in inorganic matter.

But, before discussing this, it should be asked whether we have the right to attribute the idea of life to the cell.

We say, for instance, that life resides in the cell, that this is a living being. Yet the essential idea of human life, and the idea of the life which is in the cell, are not only different, but incompatible. The one excludes the other. I learn that my body is entirely composed of cells. I am told that these cells have the same vital principle as myself and are living beings like myself. But I am only conscious of my life because I feel that I myself form, with all the cells which compose my body, a single undivided living being. Yet I am told that I am entirely composed of living cells. To what then ought I to attribute the property of life: to myself or to the cells? If I admit that the cells possess life, I must eliminate from the conception of life the principal sign of my life, the feeling that I am a separate undivided living being; but if I admit that I possess life, inasmuch as I am one separate undivided being, it is clear that I cannot attribute the same life to the cells which compose my body, and about the consciousness of which I know nothing.

Either I have life and am composed of non-living particles, called cells, or I am composed of a quantity of living cells, and the consciousness that I have of life is not life but an illusion.

We are not satisfied with saying that the cell contains something which we call a or b, but we say that the cell contains life. We say "life" because we understand under this name not some unknown x, but a well-determined quantity, which we all know equally, and which we know only by ourselves as the consciousness that we have of our body forming a single undivided being. Consequently this conception cannot refer to the cells which compose my body.

Whatever may be the researches and the observations to which a man devotes himself, he is bound, if he would show a result from them, to employ every word with a meaning admitted equally by all without dispute, and he must not attribute to it a meaning which he wishes to give it, but which does not agree with the fundamental idea generally accepted. If one might use the word "life" in such a manner as to indicate equally the nature of the whole object, and the properties of the different parts of which it is composed, as is done in the case of the cell and the animal composed of cells, then one might use other words in the same way; one might say, for instance, that ideas being expressed by words, words being composed of letters, and letters of strokes, the forming of the strokes is the same thing as the expression of ideas, therefore one might call the strokes ideas.

It is the most ordinary thing, for example in the scientific world, to hear and read of theories tending to prove that life proceeds from the play of forces physical and mechanical.

One might even say that most scientific men hold this (it is difficult to know what to call it)—opinion not an opinion, parody not a parody, but rather a jest or a riddle.

They say that life proceeds from the play of forces physical and mechanical, forces the nature of which we call physical and mechanical only in opposition to the idea of life.

It is evident that the word "life"—improperly applied to ideas foreign to it and which wander farther and farther from its essential meaning—is so entirely removed from its centre, that life is placed where, according to our conception, it cannot be. It is as if one declared that there is a circle or a sphere with the centre outside the circumference.

In fact, life, which presents itself to me solely as a tendency from evil to good, is met with in a region where there is neither good nor evil. It is evident that the centre of the conception of life has been entirely displaced; moreover, in examining the researches on those things which they call "life" I see that they include hardly any of the ideas that we are familiar with. I see a whole series of new ideas and words which have their conventional meaning in scientific language, but which have nothing in common with existing ideas.

The idea of life is not taken in the sense that all attribute to it, and in consequence of that the deductions drawn from it are also out of touch with the sense generally received; they are new arbitrary ideas for which it is necessary corresponding new words shall be invented.

Human language is more and more banished from scientific researches, and in place of words which express real objects and ideas, arises a scientific Volapük which is distinguished from the true Volapük only because the real Volapük expresses in general terms true objects and ideas, whilst the scientific Volapük designates by names which do not exist ideas which exist still less.

The only method of intellectual communication between men is that of speech; but for that communication to be possible, it is necessary to employ words in such a manner that every one of them unfailingly suggests to every man the same ideas, corresponding and exact. But if it is permitted to employ words at random, and to give to them arbitrary meanings, it would be better not to speak, but to communicate by gestures.

I admit that to settle the laws of the universe solely by deductions from reason, without experiment or observation, is to follow a false and unscientific method, a method that cannot lead to true science.

But to study the phenomena of the Universal by way of observation and experiment, allowing oneself to be guided in these experiments and these observations not by ideas generally admitted but by conventional scientific ideas, and explaining the results of these experiments by means of words to which different meanings can be attributed,—is not this still worse? The best chemist can do the greatest harm if the labels are put on the bottles, not according to their contents, but according to the whims of the chemist.

But, positive science, I may be told, does not aim at the study of the whole combination of life (comprising will, aspiration towards good and the spiritual world); it separates only from the idea of life those phenomena submitted to its experiments and investigations.

If it were thus, it would be perfectly legitimate. But we know that the savants of the present day do not understand it thus. If we admit, first of all, the conception of life in its essential meaning, which all understand, and if we establish clearly that positive science, setting aside all aspects of that conception except the one which is alone susceptible of being observed, and only examine the phenomena from this one side. while applying to it the scientific method of investigation, that would be all right, and an entirely different thing. The place that science would then have occupied and the results we should have arrived at then on the foundation of science would have been altogether different. But we must state facts, and not hide what we all know. Do we not know that the greater number, if not all, of the *savants* of positive science, in studying life are fully convinced that they are studying the whole of life and not merely one of its sides?

Astronomy, mechanics, physics, chemistry, as well as the other sciences, taken singly and all together, clear up each one the part of life which is submitted to it, without coming to any conclusion touching life generally. It was only in the period when the sciences were in their infancy, when they were not clear or well - defined, that some among them attempted to include from their standpoint all the phenomena of life, and became obscure by inventing new ideas and words. This was the case with Astronomy, when it was called Astrology, and with Chemistry, when it was called Alchemy. The same thing now happens with that experimental Science of Evolution, which, in studying one or more sides of life, professes to study the whole of life.

Men who look at science from such an erroneous point of view, refuse to recognize that their researches only include certain sides of life, but aver that all life, with all its phenomena, is to be investigated by the means of external experimentation. If Psychism, say they (they love that vague word in their Volapük), is as yet unknown to us, it will be known to us some day. By studying one or more phases of the phenomena of life, we shall come to know all. In other words, by examining attentively and for a long while one of the sides of an object, we shall succeed in seeing all the sides and even the whole of it.

However surprising such a strange doctrine may appear, which cannot be explained except as the fanaticism of superstition, it nevertheless does exist, and, like all barbarous and fanatical doctrines, it produces a pernicious influence, leading the activity of human thought in a false and vain direction.

Conscientious workers perish, having devoted their lives to the study of an almost useless thing; the material forces of people perish from being directed there where they are not necessary; young generations perish, being directed to the same vain activity of Kyfa Makëitch, elevated to the rank of the highest service of humanity.

It is customary to say that science studies all the aspects of life. But the truth is that every object has as many aspects as there are radii in a sphere, that is to say an infinite number, and that it is impossible to study them all. It is necessary to ascertain which is the most important and the most necessary, and which is of less use and less importance. Just as one cannot approach an object on all its sides at once, so one cannot study the phenomena of life on all its aspects at once. Whether we like it or not, it is only possible to study first one aspect then another. To know what we should study in the first place, what in the second place, that is the great thing. To know what it is most important to know is the " key " of science. This " key " can only be obtained by the knowledge of a true conception of life.

There is but one true conception of life which can give a true meaning and a right direction to all the sciences in general and to each one in particular, in arranging them according to their importance in relation to life. If our idea of life is not such as is implanted in us all, then all our science will be false.

What we call science cannot define life; it is, on

the contrary, our idea of life which decides what we must consider as science. Thus then, for science to be science, it is necessary to begin by resolving the question of knowing what is science and what is not, and for that it is necessary that the idea of life should be clear.

I will say frankly what I think. We all know the fundamental dogma of this false experimental science : — Matter and its energy exist. Energy produces movement ; mechanical movement is transformed into molecular movement ; molecular movement is manifested by heat, electricity, nervous and mental activity. All the phenomena of life without exception are explained by the relationship of different energies.—All this appears clear, simple, and above all convenient. So that if nothing of all this which we desire so much and which so simplifies all our life exists, then it must all be invented in some way or other.

I will express my daring, audacious thought yet more fully : — A great part of the energy, of the passionate activity of experimental science arises from the desire to invent all that is necessary to confirm so convenient an idea.

In the activity of this science one sees not so much the desire to study the phenomena of life, as a constant effort to prove the truth of its fundamental dogma. What forces are wasted in attempting to explain how the organic proceeds from the inorganic, and the activity of the soul from the processes of the organism ! But the organic does not proceed from the inorganic. " Let us search at the bottom of the sea," they say ; "we shall find there a piece of something we will. call the kernel." It is not there, but they continue to believe it is to be found. They have looked well for a fact to prove the possibility of the production of an organised being from inorganic matter. They have. not found it, but they continue to affirm it the more that they have at their services an infinite number of centuries to which they can relegate all that they ought to find now to confirm their theory, but which in reality does not exist.

It is the same with respect to' the transition of organic activity to psychic activity; there is no such thing yet. But we are determined that there shall be, and we employ all the efforts of our mind to show at least the possibility of it.

The discussions on that which does not concern life, that is to say the question of its origin (whether it be *animism, vitalism,* or some other imaginary force), have hidden from men the principal question of life, that question without which the idea of life has no meaning; and have reduced little by little the men of this so-called science, those who ought to guide the others, to the state of a man who walks on, who hurries even, but who has forgotten whither he is going.

But perhaps it is on purpose that I try not to see the immense results gained by science in its present direction? But no result can correct a false direction. Let us grant the impossible, and admit that all which contemporary science desires to learn about life, all that it affirms can be discovered (without believing it itself), granting, I say, that all this is discovered, that all is clear as the day;—it is evident, then, that organic matter proceeds from inorganic through adaptation; it is evident that physical force changes into the senses, the will, the thought; that all this is so evident that not only the professors but also the scholars in the primary schools know that such thoughts, such sentiments, proceed from such activities,—Well, what then?

Can I at will direct these activities in such a manner as to awaken in myself such or such thoughts, or can I not? The question of knowing *what* thoughts and *what* feelings I ought to awaken in myself and in others is not only not answered, it is not even touched upon.

I know that scientists will find no difficulty in replying to this question. The solution appears to them very simple, as the solution of all difficult questions appears simple to those who do not understand the question itself. The problem of how to organise life when it is in our power, appears very simple to the scientists. They say: It must be arranged in a manner which will enable men to satisfy their wants. Science will, first of all, find out how to distribute justly the wherewithal to satisfy wants; and, secondly, how to produce so much and so easily that all wants shall be satisfied without trouble,—and then everybody will be happy.

In the meantime, if one asks what is understood by wants, and how they are limited, the reply is again very simple: It is for science to classify the wants, physical, intellectual, æsthetic, even moral, and to define clearly for us those which are legitimate and those which are not, and in what measure.

But if one asks what should guide us in deciding which wants are legitimate and which are not, they reply boldly: "The *study* of these wants." But the word "wants" has only two meanings: either wants are the conditions of existence, and there is an infinite number for every object, consequently they cannot all be studied; or they are the aspiration towards good which is the proof of a living being, a want perceived and determined solely by the consciousness; consequently still less susceptible of being studied by experimental science.

Science will decide this some day. There is an institution, a body, an association of men of intelligence which is infallible, and is called science. It will define everything in time.

Is it not evident that such a solution of the

question is but a parody of the reign of the Messiah, a reign in which science plays the part of the Messiah ? For such an explanation to be accepted one must have a faith in the dogmas of science as blind as that of the Jews in the coming of the Messiah. There is but one point of difference between the faithful in science and the faithful in Israel : the orthodox Jew believing the Messiah to be God's messenger, *may* think that he will have the power to change everything for the better, whilst the orthodox scientist *cannot* believe, considering the object of his studies, that it will ever be possible for him, by the external study of wants, to solve the one great problem of life.

CHAPTER I

The essential contradiction inherent in human life.

EVERY man lives only for his own happiness, for his well-being. When he ceases to look for well-being, he no longer feels himself alive. Man cannot think of life without associating therewith the desire for his own well-being. Living is to every man synonymous with seeking for well-being and aiming at its possession; to seek for well-being and to aim at possessing, this is to live. Man has no consciousness of life but in himself, in his individuality; that is why he believes at first that the good which he desires is solely his own individual good. It seems to him at the very first that life, true life, is his own life only. The existence of other beings seems to him altogether different from his own; to his eyes theirs is but an appearance of life. Man does nothing but look at the life of other individuals, and it is only by his personal observations that he comes to the knowledge of their existence. He only knows the life of other beings when he wishes to think of it; but when it is a question of himself he knows and cannot cease for an instant to know that he lives. Consequently true life presents itself to him only under the form of his own life. The life of the beings which surround him seems to him but one of the conditions of his own existence. If he does not wish evil to others, it is only because the sight of the sufferings of others troubles his well-being. If he wishes good to others, it is also for himself; it is not that those to whom he wishes well may be happy, but only that the good of others may augment the welfare of his own life. What is important to man, what is necessary to him, is only the good of his life, that is to say his own good.

But while man is aiming solely at the attainment of his own welfare, he perceives that this welfare depends on other beings. In observing and attentively examining these other beings, he notes that all men and even the animals have the same idea of life as himself. Each of these beings has only consciousness, like himself, of its own existence and of its own well-being, considering nothing important or real but its own life, whilst he sees in the life of others only an instrument for his happiness. Man perceives that every one of those living beings, as well as himself, must be ready, for the sake of securing even the smallest addition to his own welfare, to deprive of a greater good, and even of life, all the others, including himself who is thus reasoning. And after having comprehended this, man notes that if this is so, which he cannot doubt, it is not one only or a dozen beings, but an infinite number of living creatures spread all over the world, who are ready every instant, with the aim of attaining a personal end, to destroy him, for whom alone life exists. Once grasping this idea, man sees that not only will it be difficult to obtain his own individual good without which he cannot comprehend his own life, but more, that he will be certainly deprived of it. The longer man lives, the more experience comes to confirm the justice of this reasoning. He feels that the life of this world, that life in which he participates and which is composed of individuals united among themselves, who seek to destroy and to devour each other, cannot be a happiness to him, but will assuredly be a great evil. Moreover, granting that man may be placed in conditions so advantageous that he can struggle successfully with the other beings, without peril to himself, reason and experience prove to him soon that even these phantoms of happiness, which he can snatch from life in the form of individual joys are not benefits, but, so to speak, samples of good, which are only given to him that he may feel more keenly yet the sufferings always inseparable from pleasures. The more a man advances in life, the more clearly he sees that pleasures become more and more rare, and that weariness, satiety, troubles, and sufferings go on increasing.

And this is not yet all; being conscious of the weakening of his powers and of the first attacks of decay, having before his eyes the infirmities, the old age and death of other men, he further observes that his own existence, this existence in which alone he feels life really and fully, draws nearer every moment, with every movement, to decay, old age, and death. He sees besides that his life is exposed to a thousand chances of destruction on the part of other beings in strife with him, that he is exposed to sufferings which continually increase, that indeed his life, by its very nature, is but a continual march towards death, towards that state in which must disappear, along with the individual life, all possibility of any personal advantage whatever. Man perceives that he himself, his individuality, that which to him means life, is in continual contest with the whole world, with this world against which all struggle is impossible; he perceives that he is seeking pleasures which are but phantoms of happiness and which are doomed to always end in suffering, and that he is attempting to preserve a life which cannot be preserved.

He sees that he himself, this individuality, sole moving power of his longing for good and for life, can possess neither the one nor the other; and that what he desires, happiness and life, are the sole possession of those beings who are strangers to him, whom he does not know and cannot be aware of, and of whom he cannot and will not recognize the existence. The important thing for him, the one thing necessary, that which to his eyes only has true life, his individuality, perishes and will be only bones and worms, no longer himself, whilst that which he does not want, that which has no importance in his eyes, that which he does not perceive to be alive, all this crowd of beings engaged in struggling and in supplanting one another, all this is real life, which will remain and will live for ever. So that this one life, the only one of which he has consciousness, this life, sole end of all his activity, is shown to be something delusive and impossible, whilst the life outside of him, that which is by him uncared for, unperceived, and to him unknown, is the only real life.

This of which he is unaware alone offers those advantages which he would enjoy himself. This idea does not only present itself to his mind in the hours of discouragement, because it is not an idea from which one can escape, but, on the contrary, it is a truth so evident and incontestable, that, once it presents itself to the mind of man, or if others explain it to him, he can never disburden himself of it nor efface it from his consciousness

CHAPTER II

Humanity has recognized from the earliest days the contradiction of life. Wise men who have enlightened humanity, have given to the world definitions of life explaining this intrinsic contradiction, but the Pharisees and Scribes conceal it.

THAT which presents itself in the first place to man as the sole aim of life, is the happiness of his own individuality ; but for the individuality, happiness cannot exist. And even when there may occur in his life something which resembles happiness, yet that life in which alone happiness is possible, the life of the individuality, is itself dragged irresistibly with every movement, with every breath, towards suffering, evil, death and destruction !

And this is so evident, so clear, that all men who think, young and old, educated and ignorant, must know it. This argument is so simple, so natural that it comes to the mind of every intelligent man, and humanity has known it from the most remote times.

The life of man, as an individuality, aiming only at its own particular welfare among the infinite number of similar individualities who destroy each other and annihilate themselves, that life is an evil and nonsense,—and the true life cannot be of this nature.

From the earliest times man has said this to himself, and the philosophers of India, of China, of Egypt, of Greece, and the Hebrews have spoken in the most powerful and lucid terms, on this intrinsic contradiction. From the distant past the human mind has been endeavouring to find for man a happiness of such a nature that neither the strife of beings among themselves, nor sufferings, nor death, can destroy it.

It is in bringing into view more and more clearly this happiness of man, which is sure and incapable of being destroyed by strife, suffering, or death, that consists all the advance of humanity since we have known life.

From the most remote period and among the most diverse peoples, the great teachers of humanity have revealed to men clearer and yet clearer definitions of life, explaining its intrinsic contradiction, and have pointed out to them what is for man true happiness and true life. And as in this world all

men are in the same condition, it follows that all find
the same contradiction existing between their longing for personal welfare and their consciousness of
the impossibility of attaining to it, so that all the
definitions of true happiness and consequently of
true life, taught to men by the great minds of
humanity, are identical in their very essence.

" Life is a journey and a perfecting of souls, which
will enter further and further into felicity," the
Brahmins have said from the earliest times.

" Life is the diffusion of that light which came
down from heaven for the good of humanity,"
said Confucius some six hundred years before
Christ.

" Life is the abnegation of self in order to gain
the happiness of ' Nirvana,' " said Buddha, the contemporary of Confucius.

" Life is the way of meekness and humility for
obtaining good," said another contemporary of Confucius, Lao-Tsi.

" Life is what God has breathed into the nostrils
of man so that in following His law he shall attain
the good," said the Hebrew sage.

" Life is that obedience to reason, which gives
happiness to men," said the Stoics.

" Life is the love of God and of your neighbour,
which brings happiness to man," said Christ, summing
up in his definition all those which preceded it.

Such are the definitions of life, which for thousands
of years have solved the contradiction of human life
and given it a reasonable meaning by showing men
real and indestructible happiness in place of the
unreal and elusive happiness of individuality.

One may perhaps disagree with these definitions
of life and feel that they could be expressed more
exactly, more clearly, but it is impossible not to see
that they are of such a nature that their recognition
gives to life a reasonable meaning by destroying the

3

contradiction of life, and substituting for the tendency of the individual towards an unrealisable aim one towards a good which neither sufferings nor death can destroy.

One cannot avoid seeing that these definitions, which are true in theory, are sanctioned by experience, and that millions and millions of men, who have accepted them and do accept them, have shown and do show by this fact the possibility of substituting for the longing of the individuality, for its welfare, another longing for a welfare such that neither sufferings nor death can disturb it.

But besides those who have understood and who do understand the definitions of life revealed to humanity by the great men who have shed light upon it, there always has been and there is an immense majority of men who during part of their life, sometimes even during their whole life, have lived and do live only the animal life, and not only do not understand the definitions which help to solve the contradiction of human life, but do not even see the contradiction which they solve. And there have always been and there are yet, amongst these men, other men who, in consequence of their exceptional position in the world, believe themselves called to guide humanity, and, not understanding the meaning of human life themselves, have taught and are teaching to other men the meaning of this life which they do not understand, declaring that human life is nothing else than individual existence.

These false doctors have always existed and exist still in our day. Some profess in words the doctrines of these leaders of humanity in whose traditions they have been trained ; but, being strangers to the actual meaning of those doctrines, they transform them into supernatural revelations about the past and future life of men, contenting themselves with demanding the practice of ceremonies. This is, in its largest acceptation, the teaching of the Pharisees, that is to say of men who profess that life, absurd in itself, can be amended by the belief in another life to be gained by the practice of external ceremonies.

Others, refusing to admit the possibility of any other life than that which they see, deny every kind of miracle, all that is supernatural, and declare boldly that the life of man is nothing else than his animal existence, from birth to death. Such is the doctrine of the Scribes, the people who teach that in the life of man, as well as in that of the animal, there is nothing unreasonable.

And these false doctors of both kinds, notwithstanding that their doctrines have for their basis one and the same gross ignorance of the essential contradiction of human life, have always quarrelled and quarrel still among themselves.

These two kinds of teaching are dominant in our world, and, hostile to each other, fill it with their disputes, hiding from men, behind these same disputes, those definitions of life which reveal the way of the true welfare of men, given to humanity thousands of years ago.

The Pharisees, not understanding the definition of life given to men by the masters in whose traditions they have been trained, replace it by their false interpretations of the future life, and endeavour at the same time to hide from men the definitions of life given by the other masters of humanity, presenting them to their disciples mangled in a most gross and brutal manner, believing that they will thus maintain the exclusive authority of the doctrine on which they base their interpretations.

[The unity of the reasonable meaning of the definitions of life given by the other teachers of humanity does not appear to them to be, as it ought to be, the best proof of the truth of their teaching ; because this unity, in fact, undermines confidence in their own ridiculous and false interpretations by which they replace the groundwork of the doctrine they teach.]

The Scribes, without a suspicion even of the true foundation on which the doctrines of the Pharisees have been built, reject categorically all teachings of a future life, and declare without hesitation that these doctrines rest on nothing, are but remnants of rude customs born of ignorance, and that the progress of humanity consists in not asking oneself any questions about life outside of the limits of the animal existence of man.

CHAPTER III

The errors of the Scribes.

AND, astonishing thing! this fact, that all the doctrines of the great intellects of humanity have struck men by their sublimity to such a degee that the common people have ascribed to most of them a supernatural character, and have made demi-gods of their founders,—this which is the very hall-mark of the importance of these doctrines,—it is this very circumstance which gives the Scribes the best proof, as they think, of the incorrectness and imperfection of these doctrines.

The fact that the insignificant doctrines of Aristotle, of Bacon, of Comte, and of others, have been and remain always the property of a small number of readers and admirers, that these doctrines, because of their falsity, have never been able to exercise an influence on the masses, and consequently have not undergone the alterations and amplifications which superstition produces, even this mark of their insignificance is accepted as a proof of their truth.

As for the doctrines of the Brahmins, of Buddha, of Zoroaster, of Lao-Tsi, of Confucius, of Isaiah and of Christ, they are reckoned as superstition and error, simply because they have changed root and branch the existence of millions of individuals.

The facts that billions of men have lived and do live according to these superstitions, because, even in their altered condition, they give men answers to questions on the true welfare of life, and that these doctrines not only open out, but help fundamentally the thought of the best men of all centuries, and that indeed the theories accepted by the Scribes are only circulated among themselves and are continually contested, sometimes even do not live ten years, forgotten as soon as they appear,—all these things do not trouble them in the least.

This false direction of the studies which contemporary society follows is shown in nothing more clearly than in the place occupied in this society by the doctrines of those great masters of life by which humanity has lived and been moulded, and in accordance with which it continues to live and mould itself.

In the Almanacs, in the chapter on statistics, it is stated that the number of religions professed now by the inhabitants of the terrestrial globe reaches a thousand. It is taken for granted that Buddhism, Brahmanism, Confucianism, Taoism, and Christianity are comprised in that number.

A thousand religions! And the men of our day actually sincerely believe them to be all absurd, and their study useless! Yet these same men consider it a shameful thing to be ignorant of the latest sayings of the wisdom of Spencer, of Helmholtz and others. As for the Brahmins, Buddha, Confucius, Lao-Tsi, Epictetus, Isaiah, they may sometimes know their names, but often even these are unknown to them. It never occurs to them that the number of the religions professed in our day is nothing like a thousand, but just three : the Chinese religion ; the Indian religion ; the Hebraic-Christian religion (of which Mahommedanism is a branch), or that one can buy for ten shillings and read through in two weeks. the books of these religions ; finally, that the books in accordance with which all humanity has lived and lives now, with the exception of seven per thousand of individuals who are almost unknown, contain all human wisdom, all that has made humanity what it is.

That the masses do not understand the doctrines is a small matter, but the educated classes, if they have not made them their speciality, ignore them, and the philosophers by profession do not consider it necessary so much as to glance at these books.

In fact, why study these teachers who have solved the contradiction of life known by reasonable men to exist, and who have defined the true good and the life of man ? The Scribes, not recognizing this contradiction which constitutes the principal part of the rational life, affirm positively, that as they do not see the contradiction, it does not exist, and that the life of man is limited to his animal existence.

Those who have sight understand and describe what they see before them ; the blind man goes poking with his stick and declares there is nothing outside of what is made known to him by the noise of his stick.

CHAPTER IV

The doctrine of the Scribes substitutes the visible manifestation of man's animal existence for the conception of the complete life of man, and draws from these manifestations deductions as to the aim of life.

"Life is that which takes place in a living being between its birth and its death. Man is born, the dog, the horse, are born; each has a special body; this body lives a certain time and then dies, decomposes, passes into other beings, and ceases to be. Life was, life is no more. The heart beats, the lungs act—the body does not decompose, the man, the dog, the horse, live. The heart ceases to beat, respiration is arrested — the body begins to decompose; the animal is dead; life is no more in them. Life then is that which takes place in the body of a man, as in that of an animal, in the interval of time between birth and death."

What could be clearer? It is thus that the most savage and ignorant men, scarcely raised above the animal condition, have regarded and do regard life. And actually in our own day the doctrine of the Scribes, which calls itself Science, takes this most primitive, most ignorant representation of life to be the one true representation.

By means of all those instruments of superficial knowledge which men have acquired, this false doctrine brings them back systematically to the rear, to that night of ignorance, from which it has taken so much trouble and effort, during thousands of years, to free them. We cannot define life in our consciousness, says this doctrine. We go astray when we examine it in ourselves. This conception of well-being, the search for which in our consciousness constitutes our life, is a deceptive mirage, for in this consciousness we cannot conceive of life. To understand life, it is enough to consider its manifestations exactly as one considers all movements of matter. It is only by such observations, and by the laws resulting from them, that we shall find at once the law of life in general and that of the life of man in particular.

[True science, knowing its place and, consequently, its object, is modest; and this is what gives it its power; it never speaks and never has spoken in that way.

Physics speaks of the laws and the relationships of forces without giving attention to the question what force itself is, and without attempting to explain its nature. Chemistry treats of the relationships of matter without troubling about what matter is, nor attempting to define its nature. Zoology treats of the forms of life without asking the question what life itself is, nor attempting to define its essence. And force, matter, life, are not regarded by true science as objects of study, but as the bases for the axioms of another domain of human knowledge, and on which is constructed the edifice of every separate science. It is thus that true science regards its object, and this science has never had the pernicious and brutalising influence that the false science has had. But false scientific philosophy does not thus regard its object. "Matter, force, life, we study all these; and if we study them then we can know their essence," they say, not considering that they are studying neither matter, nor force, nor life, but only their relations and forms.]

And now this false doctrine having set aside the conception of the complete life of man, the life he is conscious of, and having substituted for it the portion one sees, that is to say animal existence, sets itself to study these visible manifestations, first in man, in so far as he is animal, then in animals in general, in plants, finally in matter, asserting constantly that it is life itself which is studied, and not merely one or two of its manifestations.

The observations are so complicated, so varied, so entangled, they demand the sacrifice of so much time and work, that people forget little by little the original error (taking a part of an object for the object itself), and in the end they are completely convinced that the study of the visible properties of matter, plants, and animals, is the study of life itself,

—of that life which men can only recognize by their consciousness.

It is not unlike what takes place when a person shows something in the dark, and wishes to maintain the illusion for the spectators. "Do not look anywhere else," he says, "only where the reflection is shown; above all do not look at the object itself; even pretend to yourselves that the object does not exist, only the reflection from it." This is precisely what is done by the false science of the Scribes of our age in seeking to gain the good graces of the crowd, and contemplating life without the principal definition of its striving after happiness which is revealed only in the consciousness of man. (Appendix I.)

Starting from a definition of life which does not include the tendency towards good, the false science observes the aims of living beings, and finding among the number some aims which are foreign to man, imposes them upon him.

The preservation of the individuality, and of the species, the reproduction of similar beings, and the struggle for existence,— this is the aim of living beings according to superficial observation, and it is this same deceptive aim of life which is also imposed upon man.

False science having taken for its starting-point a worn-out representation of life where this contradiction, which is its chief characteristic, does not appear—this pretended Science, in its last deductions arrives at what the great majority of men are demanding, the recognition of the possibility of well-being for one's own personal life, and the recognition of the personal and animal existence as the only good possible to man.

False science goes even further than the demands of the common herd (demands for which it would wish to find an explanation),—it even affirms what the reasonable consciousness of man denies from the time it is manifested : the conclusion that the life of man, like that of any other animal, consists in the struggle for the existence of the individuality, of the genus, and of the species. (Appendix II.)

CHAPTER V

The false doctrines of the Pharisees and Scribes no more explain the true meaning of life than they give guidance in it. Custom without any reasonable explanation is the sole guide of life.

"It is unnecessary to define life; everyone understands it, and we already live," say the people, deceived and kept in their illusions by the false doctrines; and knowing neither what life is, nor what constitutes their well-being, it seems to them that they live, even as one who floats at the mercy of the waves without any direction seems to himself to be nearing the place where he ought to be, and wishes to be.

An infant is born in want or in luxury, and receives the education of the Pharisees or Scribes. For this child, for the youth, the contradiction in life does not exist, any more than the question of life itself exists, and this is why no explanation of the Pharisees nor of the Scribes is necessary, or can guide him. He is guided solely by the example of the people who live around him, and this example is the same, whether of Pharisees or Scribes : both live only for the good of the personal life, and they only teach the child the way to acquire this delusive good.

If the father and mother are in want, the child learns from them that the aim of life is to acquire the most bread and money with the least possible amount of work, so that the animal individuality may have all the enjoyment possible. If the child comes into the world in the midst of luxury, it learns that the aim of life is riches, honours, and the passing of time in the gayest and most agreeable way possible.

All the knowledge that the poor man acquires only serves to increase the well-being of his personality. All the knowledge acquired by the rich man in science and art, in spite of all the grand things said about the importance of science and art, are only of value to him in order to banish boredom and pass the time agreeably. The longer they both live, the more strongly do they become impregnated with the ruling ideas of the people of the world. They marry, they create a family, and the eagerness which they put into acquiring the advantages of animal life continues to increase, justified as it is by the existence of their family. The struggle with others becomes more implacable, and the habit is established of living only for the good of the individuality.

If in the spirit of either the poor man or the rich man there arises a doubt of the reasonableness of such a life, if either the one or the other puts the question : " Why this aimless struggle for my existence, which will be continued in my children, or why this deceptive pursuit of pleasures which end in suffering, the same for my children as for myself ? " —there is scarcely any probability that in reply to these questions he will be taught the definitions of life given in the past to humanity by its great masters, who found themselves, thousands of years before him, in the same conditions.

The doctrines of the Pharisees and of the Scribes so carefully hide these definitions that very few are able to see them. The Pharisees reply to the question : " Why is life miserable ? " by saying, " Life is miserable, it always has been and must always be so. The good of life is not in one's present, but in

one's past and in one's future life." The Brahmins,
Buddhists, Taoists, Hebrews, and Christian Pharisees
always say this, and only this.

"True life is an evil, and the explanation of the
evil is in the past, in the beginning of the world and
of man, whilst the reparation of the evil which exists
is in the future beyond the tomb. — All that man can
do to attain to happiness, not in this life but in that
which is to come, is to believe the doctrine that we
teach and perform the ceremonies that we ordain."

And he who doubts—seeing from the life of all
those who live for personal gratification, even from
the life of the Pharisees who live for the same end,
the fallacy of this explanation,—and stoutly refuses
to believe them, without examining deeply the
meaning of their reply, turns to the Scribes. "All
teaching concerning any other life than the animal
life which we see is born of ignorance," say the
Scribes. "All your doubts as to the reasonableness of
your life are but empty dreams. The life of the
worlds, the earth, man, the animal world, the vegetable
world, is according to laws, and we teach these laws;
we investigate the origin of the worlds, of man, of
animals, of plants, and of all matter; we investigate
also what will happen to the worlds when the sun
grows cold, etc., etc., indeed all that man and each
animal and each plant has been and will be. We can
demonstrate and prove that all has been and will be as
we say. Besides this our investigations contribute to
the amelioration of the condition of man. But of
your own life, of your aspiration towards good, we can
tell you nothing that you do not already know. You
live, and that is all; try to live as well as possible."

And he who doubts, having received no reply to
his question, either from the one side or the other,
remains as he was before, with no other guide in life
than the stimulation of his personality.

Among those who doubt, some, following Pascal's

reasoning, having said to themselves that all this may be true with which the Pharisees frighten us when we do not follow their prescriptions, carry out the commands when they have time (they will lose nothing by so doing, they say, and may reap a great advantage); others, agreeing with the Scribes, boldly deny the existence of any other life, and all religious duties, and say to themselves: "I am not the only one; everybody has lived and does live in this manner, come what may." And this difference gives no advantage to one or the other. These like the first remain devoid of any explanation of the meaning of their true life. And yet one must live.

The life of man is a series of actions from the time he awakes till he sleeps again; every day and incessantly he must choose, among the hundreds of things which he might do, those which he wishes to do. Neither the doctrine of the Pharisees which explains the mysteries of heavenly life, nor that of the Scribes which investigates the origin of worlds and of man, and decides upon their future destiny, serves to guide him in the choice of his actions. And without guide in the choice of his actions man cannot live. And you find this man whether he likes it or not yielding forthwith, not to reason, but to that external guide to life which has always existed and still exists in all human societies.

There is no reasonable explanation of this guide, and yet this it is which causes the immense majority of the actions of all men. This guide is habit, habit which dominates the most completely the men who the least understand the meaning of their life. This guide cannot be clearly defined, since it is composed of things and actions that differ according to time and place. For the Chinese it is a custom of lighting candles on the tombs of ancestors; for the Mahommedan, pilgrimages to certain places; for the Hindoo, a certain number of prayers; for the soldier, fidelity to the flag and the honour of the uniform; for the man of the world, the duel; for the mountaineer, the vendetta; it is a custom of eating certain foods on particular days; it is a certain way of bringing up one's children. It is visits to pay, a certain arrangement of one's house, certain fashions of celebrating funerals, births, and marriages; in a word, it is an infinite number of affairs and actions which fill up the whole of life. They are called "propriety," "custom," and most often "duty,"— even "sacred duty."

It is to this guide, without the explanations of life given by the Pharisees and Scribes, that the majority of men submit themselves. From infancy man sees around him people who do these things with a great deal of assurance and outward solemnity, and for want of a rational explanation of the meaning of his life, not only does he set himself to do the same things, but he tries to attribute to them a sensible meaning. He wishes to believe that the people who do these things know why they do them, and with what object.

He tries to persuade himself that these things have a sensible meaning; and that the explanation of their meaning, if not completely known to him, is clear to other people. But most of these other people, for want of a rational explanation of life, are exactly in the same position as himself. They do these things, just because they imagine that the others know their meaning, and demand that they shall do them too. And thus, by involuntarily leading one another into error, men not only more and more get into the habit of doing things that have no reasonable explanation, but they even get into the habit of thinking that they *have* some mysterious meaning, incomprehensible to themselves. And the less they understand the meaning of their actions, and the less clear these actions are to themselves, so much the more do they attach importance to them, and the greater is their solemnity in performing them. Rich and poor alike do as they see others do around them, and call it "doing their duty," their "sacred duty"; they say, for their own comfort, that actions performed for so long a time by so many people all attaching great value to them, are evidently the real business of life. To extreme old age, even to death, they try to make themselves believe that if they themselves do not know why they live other people do know: but these others are just as ignorant about the matter as those who refer it to them.

New-comers enter into existence, are born, grow up, and seeing this feverish agitation to which one gives the name of life, an agitation in which respected and honoured old men with white hair take part, they are convinced that this senseless bustle is life, and that there is no other; then they go away after jostling each other on the threshold.

It is as if a man who had never seen an assembly were to imagine that the crowd pressing so noisily and excitedly around the entrance were the assembly, and should return to his house after being jostled on the threshold, with bruised sides, yet with a full conviction that he had taken part in an assembly.

Tunnelling through mountains, voyaging round the world, electricity, the microscope, the telephone, war, parliament, philanthropy, the strife of parties, universities, learned societies, museums,—Are not all these life?

All the feverish complicated activity of men with their trade, their wars, their ways of communication, their science, their art, is for the greater part nothing more than the senseless agitation of the crowd struggling on the threshold of life.

CHAPTER VI

The division in the consciousness of the men of our time.

" VERILY, verily, I say unto you, the hour cometh, and is already come, when the dead shall hear the voice of the Son of God, and they who hear shall live." And this hour has come. In vain man has tried to persuade himself, in vain others have assured him, that life can only be happy and reasonable beyond the tomb, or that individual life alone can be happy ,and reasonable ; he cannot believe it. He feels in his inmost soul an unquenchable yearning for happy and rational life, and considers that life which has no goal but existence beyond the tomb, or the impossible well-being of his own individuality, to be an evil and an absurdity.

" Live for a future life ? " says man *to himself*. " But if this life, this mere sample of life that I know, if my present life has to be absurd, far from strengthening my belief in the possibility of another reasonable life this proves to me on the contrary that life in its very essence is an absurdity, that any other than a meaningless life there cannot be.

" Live for oneself ? But my individual life is an evil and an absurdity. Live for one's family ? For the community ? For one's country ? For humanity even ? But if my individual life is unhappy and absurd, the same may be said of the life of all other human individualities. .Consequently the grouping together of an infinite number of absurd and unreasonable individualities can never form one single happy and reasonable life. Live in isolation, not knowing wherefore, doing as others do ? But I know that others cannot tell any more than I can why they do what they do."

The time is come when the reasonable consciousness begins to rise above these false doctrines and
man stops himself in the midst of life to demand
explanations. (Appendix III.)

None but the man who has no connection with
people leading a different kind of life from his own,
and he whose whole strength is used in the perpetual
struggle with nature to sustain his physical existence,
can believe that doing senseless things which they
call their duty is really the actual duty of their
life.

The time is coming, it has already come, when
the imposture which offers us a verbal negation of the
present life with the aim of preparing for a future
state, and the recognition of a personal animal
existence as life, and a so-called duty as the business
of life,—the time has come, I say, when this imposture
becomes apparent to the majority of men; when
none but the people crushed by want, or brutalised
by a voluptuous life, can go on living without feeling
the absurdity and misery of their existence.

Men wake up more and more frequently at the
voice of the reasonable consciousness, they come
to life in their graves, and the essential contradiction
of human life, in spite of all men's efforts to hide
it from themselves, is manifested to the greater part
of humanity with a terrible force and clearness.

"My whole life is the seeking after my own well-
being," says man to himself on awakening, "but
my reason tells me that this well-being cannot exist
for me, and that, whatever I do, whatever I succeed
in obtaining, all will end in the same way, in suffering, death, and destruction. I want happiness, I
want life, I want what is reasonable, but I find
within me and in all around me only evil, death,
and nonsense. What is to become of me? How
can I live? What must I do?"

He receives no reply. He looks around, searching

4

for an answer to his question, and finds it not. He
finds around him doctrines which answer questions
that he never asks; but nowhere in the world
around him is there any answer to his own question.
He only finds the same unrest among people who do
without knowing why what others do also knowing
still less why. Everyone lives as if he were unaware
of the misery of his condition and the want of reason
in his activities. "They are out of their senses, or
else I am," says the man who is awakening. "But
they cannot all be mad, it must therefore be myself.
But no, this reasonable self which tells me this cannot
be mad. Although it stand alone against the whole
world, I cannot but believe it."

And the man recognizes himself alone in the
world face to face with these terrible questions
which torture his soul. Yet he has to live.

One self, his individuality, orders him to live.
While his other self, his reason, says to him: "It
is impossible to live."

The man feels himself cut in two, and his soul is
tormented by this division. His reason seems to
him the cause of this division and of this suffering.
The Reason of man, this higher faculty indispensable
to his life, which gives to him, a naked, helpless
creature in the midst of the destructive forces of
nature, the means of existence and of enjoyment, it
is precisely this faculty which poisons his life.

In all the world which surrounds him, among
living beings, the faculties which belong to these
beings are indispensable to them, are common to all
and contribute to their happiness. The plants, the
insects, the animals, in submitting to their own law
live a happy, joyous, and serene life. And behold,
in man, this higher faculty, a part of his very nature,
produces in him a condition so pitiable that often
(more and more frequently in our time) he cuts the
Gordian knot of his life and kills himself only to

escape from the cruel inner contradiction produced by his reasonable consciousness which in our days has attained its highest degree of intensity.

CHAPTER VII

The division of consciousness proceeds from the confusion of the animal life with the human.

It is simply because man regards as life that which never has been, is not, and never will be life, that it seems to man at the moment of the awakening of his reasonable consciousness that his life is torn to pieces and arrested.

Having been placed, and having grown up in the midst of the false doctrines of our age, which have led him to the conviction that life is nothing else but his individual existence, which commenced at his birth, man imagines that he began to live when he was a baby, and that his life has continued from youth to mature age. It seems to him that he has lived a great number of years without any interruption; and suddenly there comes a day when he sees clearly, it is proved to him, that it is henceforth impossible to live as he has lived up to this day, and that his life is arrested and torn to pieces.

The false doctrine has confirmed him in the idea that his life is the interval of time from birth to death. In considering the visible life of the animals he has confused the conception of this visible life with his consciousness, and is fully convinced that this visible life is in fact his real life.

But his awakened reasonable consciousness produces wants that his animal nature cannot satisfy, and he understands the folly of his previous ideas concerning life. Nevertheless the false doctrine with which he is imbued prevents him from recognizing wherein is his mistake. He cannot cease to regard life as an animal existence. It seems to him simply that the awakening of the reasonable consciousness has interrupted his life. But what he calls his life, that which seems to him to be interrupted, has never existed. What he calls his life, his existence from birth, has never been his life. The idea that he has lived all the time—from birth to the present moment, is an illusion of the consciousness like what one experiences in a dream. Up to the time of awakening there were no dreams : they are all formed at the moment of awakening. Before the awakening of the reasonable consciousness there was no life at all. The conception of his past life was produced at the moment when he awoke to reasonable consciousness.

During infancy man lived like an animal, without having any idea of life. If he had only lived for ten months he would never have become conscious of his life, nor of the life of any other being. It would have been as if he had died in his mother's womb. And what is true of the infant is equally true of the man who has been deprived of reason and of the perfect idiot, for they cannot have consciousness of their life nor of that of other beings ; and therefore they do not live a really human life. Human life only begins at the moment when the reasonable consciousness manifests itself. It is this, in fact, which reveals to man simultaneously both his present and past life, other people's lives, and all that inevitably results from the relations of these individualities, that is to say sufferings and death, these conditions of life which bring men to deny the good of individual life and to perceive the contradiction of this life which seems to stop it ﹅

Man wishes to define his life by its duration, as he can do in the case of his visible bodily existence, and suddenly a life awakens in him which does not coincide with the date of his carnal birth, and he does not wish to believe that life is just that which cannot be defined by time.

But however much a man seeks in the duration of time for a point which he might consider as the commencement of his rational life, he will never find it.

[Nothing is more common than to hear arguments on the origin and development of human life and of life in general in the duration of time. To people discussing thus, it appears that they are on the solid ground of reality, whereas there is nothing more fantastic than their arguments on the evolution of life in time. It is as if a man wishing to measure a line, instead of starting from the known point which he occupies, should, on an endless line, at various and arbitrary distances from himself, select imaginary points, and then measure the distance between these points and himself. Is it not thus that people behave who debate about the origin and development of life in man? Where, indeed, can we find on this infinite line, which represents the development of human life in the past, this arbitrary point that we must start from if it were possible to begin the fantastic history of the evolution of this life? Shall we start from the birth of the child, or his conception, or that of his parents, or, going further back, the primitive animal, the protoplasm, or the original fragment which detached itself from the sun? All these reasonings are in the region of pure fancy, it is measuring without a measure.]

Man will never find in his memory this point, this beginning of his reasonable consciousness. It seems to him that it has always been within him. If he finds something analogous to the origin of this consciousness it is not, at all events, in his carnal birth, but in a region having nothing in common

with this carnal birth.   His rational birth appears
to him under a quite different aspect from his carnal
birth.   When a man questions himself on the origin
of the reasonable consciousness, he never thinks of
himself, of his reasonable being, as the son of his
father and mother, the grandson of his paternal or
maternal grand-parents, born in such a year ; but,
setting aside all idea of any relationship, he feels
identified with the consciousness of reasonable
beings separated from him by time and space,
people who lived thousands of years before him at
the other end of the world.   He cannot even
discover traces of his own origin in his reasonable
consciousness, but he feels the link which unites
him, outside of time and space, to other reasonable
consciousnesses, as if they enter into him, or as if he
enters into them.   It is because of the awakening
in man of the reasonable consciousness that it seems
to him that this appearance of life which misguided
men take to be true life comes to an end ; misguided
men think that their life is stopping just when it is
awakening.

CHAPTER VIII

*The division and the contradiction are only apparent : they
are the consequence of false doctrine.*

THE unhappy state of division to which men are
brought when the reasonable consciousness appears
in them, is produced by a false doctrine concerning
human life regarded as animal existence from birth
to death, a doctrine in which men grow and harden.

It seems to a man who finds himself in this error
that his life is divided within him.

He knows that life is one, and he is conscious of
two lives.   When one rolls a marble between two
fingers crossed one over the other, one feels the

sensation of two marbles, although one knows there is only one. The man who is imbued with a false idea of life experiences something similar.

Man's reason takes a wrong direction. He has been taught to regard as life something that is not life at all, to recognize as life the carnal existence of his personality.

And now with this false idea of an imaginary life, man beholds his life and perceives that there are two lives, the one which he has imagined, and that which actually exists.

In the eyes of such a man, the renunciation of personal well-being and the need of another well-being formulated by the reasonable consciousness are something unhealthy and unnatural. But for man, in so far as he is a reasonable being, the renunciation of the possibility of individual welfare and of personal life is an inevitable consequence of the conditions of the individual life and of the very nature of the reasonable consciousness which is united to him. The renunciation of well-being and of the individual life is, for a reasonable being, a function of his life, as natural as for a bird to use its wings to fly instead of running with its feet. If the little bird, although covered with feathers, uses its feet, that is no proof that it is not its nature to fly. If we still see around us men whose consciousness is not yet awakened, and who are placing their life in their individual happiness, that is no proof that it is not the nature of man to live the rational life. If the awakening to true life, the life natural to man, is brought about in our age with so grievous an effort, it is because the false teaching of the world strives to convince men that the indication of life is the life itself, and that the manifestation of the true life is nothing else than the violation of its law.

Men of our time, who are entering into the true life, are, so to speak, situated like a girl who is ignorant of the feminine nature. At the first appearance of the signs of womanhood she looks upon this condition, which leads her towards future family life, towards the duties and joys of maternity, as an unhealthy and unnatural condition, and it brings her to despair.

Men in our days experience a similar despair at the first symptoms of their awakening to the true human life. The man in whom the reasonable consciousness is awakened, but who still looks at his life from an individual point of view, finds himself in the same unhappy condition as an animal which, taking life to consist in the movement of matter, should not recognize the law governing his individuality, and should have no idea of life except as submission to the laws of matter, which act without its efforts. This animal would experience a cruel inward contradiction and division. Conforming only to the one law of matter, it would believe life to consist in lying down and breathing,—while its individuality would demand something more : nutrition and the reproduction of the species ; thus it would seem to the animal that it experienced a division and a contradiction. Life, according to it, should consist in obeying the law of gravity, that is to say not to move, but to lie down, and to undergo those chemical changes which take place in the body, and nevertheless, while doing this, it is compelled to move, to take nourishment, and to seek for its mate.

The animal would suffer, and would feel in this state a cruel contradiction and division. This is what happens to a man who is in the habit of considering the lower law of his life, his animal individuality, as the real law of his life. The higher law of his being, the law of his reasonable consciousness, demands something else from him ; but all the life around him, as well as the false doctrines, hold him bound in this illusion, and he feels the contradiction and the division.

But just as the animal, if it would cease to suffer, must recognize as the law of its life not the inferior law of matter, but the law of its individuality, and fulfilling it, profit by the law of matter for the satisfaction of the aims of its individuality; so the awakened man has to recognize his life, not in the lower law of individuality, but in the higher law which he finds in his reasonable consciousness, and which includes this first law; then, the contradiction will disappear; his individuality will freely submit itself to the reasonable consciousness and will serve him.

CHAPTER IX

The birth of the true life in man.

In examining life in time, and in observing its appearance in the human being, we ascertain that the true life is from the first enclosed in man as in the grain of corn, and that a time arrives when it shows itself. The manifestation of the true life consists in this, that the animal individuality compels man to seek for his own happiness, while the reasonable consciousness points out to him the impossibility of individual happiness, and indicates another. Man seeks to discover this happiness which is indicated in the distance, but, unable to perceive it, he cannot believe in it at all at first, and returns to his individual well-being. Yet the reasonable consciousness which gives him just a vague glimpse of his true happiness, shows him in so unmistakable and so convincing a manner the impossibility of individual well-being, that man renounces it again, and seeks once more for this new happiness which is pointed out to him. He does not yet clearly see this rational happiness, but his individual happiness is so completely destroyed that he sees the impossibility of continuing to live his individual existence, and he begins to build up in himself a new relationship between his animal and his reasonable consciousness.

Man begins to be born to the true human life. Then something happens analogous to what takes place at every birth in the material world. The new being is born, not because it wishes to be born, nor because it pleases it, nor even because it knows it is a good thing to be born, but because it has come to maturity, and cannot continue its former existence; it must follow the course of its new life, not at all because this new life calls it, but because its former existence has become impossible.

The reasonable consciousness is developed insensibly in man's individuality; taking on such proportions, that its life in the individuality becomes impossible. Then appears a phenomenon identical with that which takes place in the germination of all things: the same destruction of the seed in the form it had until now, and the appearance of a new germ; the same apparent struggle of the preceding form of the seed which is decomposing, and the growth of the germ; the same nutrition of the germ at the expense of the seed which is decomposing.

For us, the difference between the birth of the reasonable consciousness and visible carnal germination lies in this: whilst in carnal germination in time and space we see what is evolved from the germ, the cause, the date and the conditions of this birth, whilst we know that this seed is a fruit, that under certain conditions there will come from it a plant, that this will have in its turn a flower and afterwards a fruit similar to the seed (under our very eyes is thus carried on all the evolution of life), in the case of the birth of the reasonable consciousness we perceive neither the development nor the evolution. We do not see the growth of reasonable consciousness. and its evolution because it is we who accomplish it ourselves; our life is nothing else than the birth in us of the invisible being; it is for this reason that we cannot see it. We cannot distinguish the birth of this new being, this new relationship between the reasonable consciousness and the animal consciousness, just as the seed cannot see the growth of its own stalk. When the reasonable consciousness emerges from the hidden state and appears in us, it seems to us that we experience a contradiction. But there is in reality no more a contradiction than in the case of the germinating seed. In the germinating seed we see that the life which before was in the envelope of the seed is now found in its germ. So in the man whose reasonable consciousness is awakened there is no contradiction, there is simply the birth of a new being, of a new relationship between the reasonable consciousness and the animal.

So long as a man lives without being aware that other people live also, without having learnt that pleasures can never satisfy him, and that he will die, he is not even aware that *he* lives; and thus there is no contradiction in him.

But when he has observed that other individualities are of the same nature as himself, that sufferings menace them, when he realises that his existence is a slow death, when the reasonable consciousness has produced the decomposition of the individual existence, then he can no longer place his life in that individuality in a state of decomposition, he is obliged to transfer it to this new life which is opening before him; and then there is no contradiction, as there is none in the seed which has produced a germ, and which for that reason has become decomposed.

CHAPTER X

Reason is the law recognized by man, in conformity with
which his life must be perfected.

THE true life of man, which shows itself in the
relationship between his reasonable consciousness
and his animal consciousness, begins only when he
begins to renounce the well-being of his animal
individuality.   And this renunciation begins only
when his reasonable consciousness is awakened.   But
what is this reasonable consciousness?   The Gospel
according to John begins by saying that the Word,
the "Logos" (Logos means Reason, Wisdom, Word),
is the beginning, that all is in him and all proceeds
from him; consequently Reason, this which determines all the rest, cannot in any way be defined.
    Reason cannot be defined, and we have no need
to define it, for not only do we all know it, but we
know nothing but reason.   In our relationships one
with another we are convinced beforehand, more
than of any other thing, that reason is equally
obligatory for us all.   We are all convinced that
reason is the sole basis which unites all living beings.
    There is nothing we know with more certainty
than reason.   This knowledge precedes all others.
So that all we know in the world, we know only by
virtue of its conformity to the laws of this reason,
which we know in a most unmistakable manner.
We know reason and cannot ignore it.   Indeed
reason is the law according to which reasonable
beings, that is to say men, must necessarily live.
Reason for man is that law in conformity with which
his life is perfected.   It is a law analogous to that
of the animal, according to which it feeds and
reproduces its species; like the law of growth and
efflorescence in herb and tree, as also the law of the

heavenly bodies, by which the earth and stars move. The law we feel in ourselves, which we know to be the law of our life, is the law ruling all the external phenomena of the world ; the only dif erence being that within ourselves we regard it a ı the law to which we ought to submit, whereas in external phenomena we regard it as the law of that which is accomplished without our participation. Our whole knowledge of the world is summed up in this submission to the law of reason, of which we witness the manifestation outside of ourselves in the heavenly bodies, in animals and plants, and in the whole. universe. In the external world we see this submission to the law of reason ; in ourselves we recognize it as the law which we ought to obey.

The ordinary error about life consists in this, that we mistake for the law of human life the law to which our animal body yields a visible submission, but which does not proceed from us, since our body obeys its law by itself as involuntarily as the tree, the stone, the stars obey. But the law of *our* life, that is to say the submission of our animal nature to reason, is an invisible law, invisible because it is not yet accomplished, but is in process of accomplishment by us in our life. It is only in the fulfilment of this law, that is to say in the submission of our animal nature to the law of reason, in view of the attainment of happiness, that our life consists. Not understanding that our happiness and our life consist in the submission of our animal individuality to the law of reason ; making all our life to consist in the happiness and the existence of this animal individuality, and refusing the task which has been assigned to us, we deprive ourselves of our true happiness and of our true life, and substitute for them the visible existence of our animal activity which acts independently of us and therefore cannot be our life.

CHAPTER XI

False direction of knowledge.

THE error which consists in taking for the law of
our life the law we see working in our animal
individuality, is an old error into which men have
frequently fallen and do still fall.   This error hides
from men the principal object of their knowledge,
that is to say the subordination of the animal
individuality to reason with the view of obtaining
the good of life, and substitutes for it the study of
human existence independently of the good of life.

Instead of studying the law to which the animal
individuality of man ought to submit to obtain
happiness, instead of studying all the other
phenomena of the world after having learnt this
fundamental law, false science directs its efforts
solely towards the study of the animal existence and
well-being of man, setting aside the chief object of
knowledge, which is the subordination of the animal
individuality of man to the law of reason in order
to obtain the good of the true life.

The false science, neglecting this principal object
of science, turns its energies towards the study of
the animal existence of mankind in the past and in
the present, and towards the study of the conditions of
existence of man in general in so far as he is animal.
It imagines that these studies will guide it to the
discovery of the good of human life.

The false science argues in the following manner :
"Men live now and have lived before us ; let us
see what their life has been, what changes it has
experienced in time and space, and where these
modifications lead to.   From these historical changes
we shall find the law of their life."

Neglecting the principal aim of knowledge, the

study of the law of reason to which the individuality of man ought to submit for the sake of his happiness, the pretended scientists of this class, by the very end which they propose in their study, confess the uselessness of their study. In fact, if the existence of men changes only in accordance with the general laws of their animal existence, the study of those laws that govern it is quite useless and foolish.

Whether men do or do not know the law of the modification of their existence, this law operates in exactly the same manner as that which acts in the life of the moles and beavers, according to those conditions in which they are found. But if it is possible for man to arrive at the knowledge of the law of reason which should govern his life, it is clear that he can only get this knowledge where it is within his reach, that is, in his reasonable conscious-ness. Consequently, however much men study the past existence of man as an animal, they will never learn more about this existence, about what has happened to humanity, than they would have known equally well without this study. And in spite of all their researches on the animal existence of man, they will never know the law which should regulate this animal existence of man to attain the happiness of life.

This is one category of the useless theories on life which are called historical and political sciences.

There is another category of these theories, very much in vogue in these days, which completely loses sight of the one object of knowledge. "In taking man for the subject of our investigations," say the scientists, "we see that he eats, develops, reproduces his species, grows old and dies like every other animal; but there are certain psychic phenomena" (this is what they call them) "which upset our exact calculations and present too great a complexity; this is why, if we would better under-

stand man, we must first study life in its simpler
manifestations, such as those that we see in animals
and plants, which are devoid of this psychic
activity. With this intention we must observe the
life of animals and plants in general. In considering animals and plants, we see appear in them
the laws of matter which are still more simple and
which are common to all. But, since the laws of
animal life are simpler than those of human life,
those of plants still more simple, and those of matter
simpler than all the others, we must firmly establish
the investigations on what is simplest of all, namely
the laws of matter. We see that what takes place
in plants and animals takes place equally in man,"
say they; "consequently we conclude that all
that takes place in man finds its explanation in the
phenomena of the more rudimentary inanimate
matter, which we can see and submit to experimentation, and the more so since all the parts of human
activity are constantly subject to those forces which
act in matter. Every change of the matter of
which man's body is composed, modifies and disturbs
all his activity." This is why they conclude that
the laws of matter are the causes of man's activity.
They are not at all disconcerted by the idea that
there is in man something that we see neither in
animals nor plants, nor in inanimate matter, and
that this something is the only thing worth knowing,
that without which everything is futile.

They never think that if a modification of matter
in man's body disturbs his activity, it merely proves
that this modification is one of the reasons of the
disturbance of the activity of man, but it does not
prove that the movement of matter is the cause of
man's activity. Thus the harm done to the plant
when we remove the soil from under its roots, proves
that the soil may be removed at will, but not that
the plant was produced by the soil. And they study

in man the same phenomena as in inanimate matter, the plant, and the animal, supposing that the knowledge of the laws which govern the phenomena of human life can explain this life itself.

To understand the life of man, that is to say the law to which his animal individuality ought to be in subjection to obtain its well-being, men examine . either the history, but not the life, of man, or the subjection of animal, plant, and matter to diverse laws, a subjection which man perceives without having the consciousness of it in himself; in a word, they act like people who might study the position of unknown objects in order to find the way to an unknown destination which they must follow.

It is quite justifiable to say that the knowledge of the visible manifestation of human existence in history may be instructive for us, just as the study of the laws of the animal individuality of man and other animals may be instructive for us, and also the study of those laws to which matter itself is subjected. This study is important for man because it shows him, as it were in a mirror, what is certainly accomplished in his life ; but it is evident that the knowledge of what already takes place under our eyes, however complete it may be, can never give us the principal knowledge, that which we stand in need of, that is, the knowledge of the law to which our animal individuality ought to be in subjection for our good. The knowledge of the laws, in course of being carried out, is instructive for us only when we admit the law of reason to which our animal individuality ought to be in subjection, not when we fail to recognize this law.

However well a tree might study (if it were capable of it) all the phenomena of chemistry and physics which take place in it, it could in no way deduce from these observations and from this knowledge the necessity of collecting and distribut-

5 .

ing the juices for the growth of its trunk, leaves, flowers, and fruit.

Just so man, however well he may know the law governing his animal individuality and the laws governing matter, will never gather from these laws the slightest indication of what use he ought to make of the piece of bread which he holds in his hand. Ought he to give it to his wife, to a stranger, or to a dog, or should he eat it himself? Should he save this piece of bread or give it to him who asks for it? And yet human life consists only in the solution of these questions and others like them.

The study of the laws governing the existence of animals, plants, and matter is not only useful but indispensable for explaining the law of human life, but only on the condition that this study has for its aim the principal object of human knowledge : the explanation of the law of reason.

In supposing that man's life is his animal existence only, that the good revealed by the reasonable consciousness cannot be obtained, and that the law of reason is but a phantom, such study becomes not only foolish but fatal, because it hides from man the one object of his learning and confirms him in this error of thinking that by studying the reflected image of an object one may come to know that object. He who abandons himself to such a study is like a man who should study attentively all the modifications and movements of the shadow of a living being, in the belief that the cause of the movement of the living being was contained in the modifications and the movements of its shadow.

CHAPTER XII

The cause of false knowledge is the false perspective in
which objects appear.

"TRUE knowledge," said Confucius, "consists in
knowing that which we know, and not knowing
that which we do not know."

False knowledge consists in thinking we know what
we do not know, and that we know not what we do
know ; and it is impossible to give a more exact definition of the false knowledge which reigns among us.
The false science of our day takes for granted that
we know what we cannot know, and that we cannot
know the only thing we really do know. Under the
influence of false knowledge, man imagines that he
knows all that appears before him in space and time,
and that he does not know what is known to him
by his reasonable consciousness.

Such a man imagines that good in general, and
his good in particular, are things he cannot understand at all. His reason, his reasonable consciousness, seem to him also to be incomprehensible. He
believes he has a notion, a little more exact, of himself as an animal. Animals and plants seem to him
still easier to understand. But what he thinks he
understands best is the inanimate matter displayed
all around him. Something similar happens with
man's sight. Without knowing why, instinctively, man
always chooses to turn his attention towards the most
distant objects, that is towards those whose form and
colour seem to him the simplest : the sky, the horizon,
the distant plains and forests. The more distant
these objects are the simpler and better defined they
appear to be : whereas the nearer you come to them
the more complicated their form and colour appear.

If man could not tell how to judge the distance

of the objects, if he neglected in looking at them to arrange them according to perspective, if he took extreme simplicity and definiteness of form and colour in an object for the supreme degree of visibility, the unbounded sky would seem to be the simplest and the most visible of all things for such a man. The more complicated lines on the horizon would seem less distinct than the sky. The houses and trees having still more intricate form and colour would seem still less visible. His hand held before his eyes would appear less visible again. Finally, the light would seem to be the least visible. Is it not thus with the false teaching of man? His reasonable consciousness, which he knows with most certainty, seems to him beyond the reach of his understanding, because it is not simple. While, on the contrary, unlimited and eternal matter, which is really beyond the reach of his understanding, seems to him the easiest thing there is to understand; its remoteness from himself making it appear simple.

But just the contrary of this is the case. First of all every man can know, and does know with certainty, the good to which he aspires; in the second place he knows equally well, reason, which indicates to him this good. He knows also his animal nature subjected to this reason. Lastly, he sees, without understanding, all the other phenomena appearing to him in time and space.

Only a man with a wrong understanding of life can imagine that he knows objects the better the more precisely they are defined by time and space. In reality we know completely only what is not defined either by time or space: good, and the law of reason. But the objects outside ourselves we know the less the less our consciousness participates in their cognition; consequently all that can be defined of an object is its position in time and space. Therefore the more an object is defined by time and space exclusively the less it is accessible to man's understanding (the less can he understand it).

Man's true knowledge terminates at the cognition of his own personality, of his animal self. Man knows this animal self, which is striving towards good and is subjected to the law of reason, quite apart from this knowledge of all that is not his personality. He knows himself really in this animal, and knows himself thus not because he is a thing of time and space (far from this, he can never know himself as a manifestation of time and space), but because he is something which is forced to submit to the law of reason to obtain its good. He is conscious of himself in this animal as something independent of time and space. When he asks himself what position he occupies in time and space it always seems to him that he stands in the very centre of an infinite period, without beginning or end, and that he is the centre of a sphere whose surface is everywhere and nowhere. What a man knows with certainty is this self which is outside of time and space, and this self, this " I," is the limit of his actual knowledge. He is ignorant of everything outside this self, and can only observe it and judge of it in an external and conditional manner.

If man renounces for a time this knowledge of himself as a reasoning centre striving towards good, that is to say as a being independent of time and space, he may for a time admit conditionally that he is a part of the visible world manifested in time and space. In thinking of himself as in time and space in relation with other beings, man joins together the true and inward consciousness of himself, and the external observation of this same self, and thus obtains an idea of himself as a man in general resembling all other men. By means of this conditional knowledge of himself, he obtains an external idea of other men, but he does not know them.

The impossibility he finds of getting a real knowledge of men comes also from his seeing not one only, but hundreds and thousands. He is aware too that there have lived and still live men whom he has never seen and never will see.

Beyond men, farther away still from himself, man sees in time and space animals which differ from men and from one another. These beings would be absolutely incomprehensible to him if he did not possess some knowledge about man in general. But, by means of this knowledge, and by separating the reasonable consciousness from the idea of man, he arrives at a certain representation of the animals, but this representation resembles knowledge even less than his representation of men in general. He sees an innumerable host of the most varied animals, and the more numerous they are the harder evidently it is for him to know them. Farther away still, he sees plants. The number of these phenomena spread through the universe is still greater, so that the impossibility of knowing them is increased.

Farther away still, beyond animals and plants, in time and space, man sees lifeless bodies, and forms of matter differing little or not at all one from another. Matter he understands least of all. His knowledge of the forms of matter is altogether indistinct. Not only does he not know it, he can only imagine it; all the more so since matter already seems to him to be endless in extension and duration.

CHAPTER XIII

The possibility of understanding objects increases not in proportion to their manifestation in time and space, but rather by reason of the unity of the law governing the objects we are studying, and ourselves.

WHAT could be more intelligible than these expressions: The dog is in pain; the calf is affectionate—

he loves me; the bird is joyful; the horse is frightened; a good man; a vicious animal? These words, so important and so intelligible, are none of them defined by time and space; on the contrary, the less we understand the law that governs a phenomenon, the more clearly is it defined by time and space. Who can say that he understands the law of gravitation which governs the movements of the earth, the moon, and the sun? And yet an eclipse of the sun is determined with great precision in time and space.

We do not know fully anything except our own life, our aspiration towards good, and reason, which reveals to us this good. The knowledge which occupies the second place in order of certainty is that of our animal personality aspiring to its well-being and in subjection to the law of reason. In the knowledge of our own animal personality we soon see appear conditions of time and space, visible, tangible, observable, but beyond the reach of our intelligence. The knowledge which comes next in order of certainty is that of such animal personalities having the same nature as ourselves, in which we recognize the same aspirations towards good and the same reasonableness as in ourselves. The more nearly the life of these individualities approaches the laws of our life, aspiration towards good and submission to the law of reason, the better do we understand it; the more it is manifested in the conditions of time and space, the less do we understand it. Thus we know best man. The knowledge that comes next in order of certainty is knowledge of animals, in whom we see an individuality aspiring to well-being like our own; but already we have difficulty in recognizing in them anything analogous to our reasonable consciousness, and it is impossible to communicate with them by means of this reasonable consciousness After animals we see

plants, and in them we can hardly recognize an individuality like our own and aspiring towards good.
These beings appear to us chiefly in their relationships of time and space, and therefore they are so
much less accessible to our understanding.

We understand them only in so far as we see in
them an individuality similar to our own animal
individuality, and in so far as this individuality, the
same as our own, aspires to good and subjects matter
to the law of reason, which is manifested in it in the
conditions of time and space.

Impersonal and material objects are still farther
removed from our understanding ; we do not find in
them a reflection of our own individuality ; we
cannot discover here any aspiration to good ; we see
nothing but the manifestation in time and space of
the laws of reason by which they are governed.

The certainty of our knowledge does not depend
upon the possibility of observing the objects in time
and space ; on the contrary, the more the manifestation of the object is capable of being observed in
time and space the less we can conceive of it.

Our knowledge of the world results from the
consciousness that we have of our aspiration towards
good, and of the necessity of submitting our animal
nature to reason in order to attain to this good. If
we understand the life of the animal, it is simply
because we see in it also aspiration to good and the
necessity of submitting to the law of reason, which
is the law of its organism.

If we do understand matter, although its good is
beyond our comprehension, it is solely because we
see taking place in it the same phenomenon as in
ourselves,—the necessity of submitting to the law of
reason, which governs it.

Knowledge, of whatever it may be, is, for us, the
bringing to bear on other objects of our knowledge
that life is an aspiration towards good, which we

can only attain by şubmitting ourselves to the law of reason.

It is an error to believe that we can arrive at the knowledge of ourselves by knowing the laws which govern animals; on the contrary, we can only know animals by means of the law that we know in ourselves. And it is a still greater mistake to believe that we can come to know ourselves by applying to our life the law of the phenomena of matter. All that man knows of the external world he knows only because he knows himself, and because he finds in himself three different relationships with the world: one a relationship of his reasonable consciousness; another a relationship of his animal; and third, a relationship of the matter of which his animal body is composed. He perceives in himself these three different relationships; and therefore all that he sees in the world groups itself always before him into a perspective composed of three planes distinct one from another: 1st, Reasoning beings; 2nd, Animals and Plants; 3rd, Inanimate Matter.

Man sees always in the world these three categories of objects, because he contains in himself these three objects of knowledge. He knows himself, firstly, as reasonable consciousness governing the animal; secondly, as animal in subjection to the reasonable consciousness; thirdly, matter in subjection to the animal.

It is not from the knowledge of the laws of matter, as people think, that we can learn the law of organisms, neither from the knowledge of the law of organisms can we know ourselves as reasonable consciousness, but *vice versâ*. First of all we can and must know ourselves, that is to say, know the law of reason to which for our good our individuality must be subjected; it is then only that we can and must gain a knowledge of the law of our animal individuality and of other individualities like it, and then, at a still greater distance from us, the laws of matter.

It is necessary for us to know, and we can know only, ourselves. The animal kingdom is to us but the reflection of what we know in ourselves. The material world is no more, so to speak, than the reflection of a reflection.

The laws of matter seem specially clear to us only because they are uniform in our eyes; they seem to be uniform for us because they are very far removed from the law of our life, the law of which we have consciousness. The laws of organisms seem to us more simple than the law of our life, also in consequence of their distance from us. But in these organisms we only observe the laws and we cannot know them as we know the law of our reasonable consciousness, which we have to fulfil.

We do not really know either the one or the other of these existences, we only see and observe what is outside of ourselves. It is only the law of our reasonable consciousness that we know in a sure and certain way, because it is necessary for our good and by it we live; but we do not see it because we cannot place ourselves at any higher point from whence to observe it.

Only if there were higher beings, dominating our reasonable consciousness, as this dominates our animal individuality, and as the animal individuality (the organism) dominates matter — these higher beings would be able to perceive our reasonable life as we perceive our animal existence and the existence of matter.

Human life appears to us indissolubly bound to two aspects of existence which are contained within it: namely, the existence of animals and plants (organic life) and that of matter.

Man himself makes his own true life, and he must

live it himself; but in these two aspects of existence united to his life man cannot take part. The body and the matter constituting him exist of themselves. These aspects of existence appear to man, so to speak, as former lives already run out, enclosed in his own life—as relics of past lives. In the true life of man, these two aspects of existence furnish him with the instrument and the materials of his work, but not with the work itself.

It is useful for man to study the materials and the instrument of his work. The better he knows them, the better he will be in a condition to work. The study of these aspects of existence contained in his life, that of his animal and that of the matter of which it is made, shows man, as in a mirror, the law which is common to all existence, that is submission to the law of reason, and, consequently, confirms him in the necessity of submitting his animal self to its law; but man cannot and must not confuse the materials and the instrument of his work with the work itself.

However much a man may have studied the visible, palpable life which he observes in himself and in others,—this life which is lived without effort on his part,—this life will always remain a mystery to him. He will never from these observations understand this life, of which he is not conscious. Never can his observations of this mysterious life, which ceaselessly vanishes from before his eyes in the infinitude of time and space, throw light upon his true life, the life which is revealed to him in his consciousness, and which consists in the subjection of his animal individuality, which is perfectly distinct from all other individualities known to him, to a quite special law of reason which he knows, as a means to attaining an entirely special good known to himself.

CHAPTER XIV

The true human life is not that which is lived in time
and space.

MAN knows life in himself as an aspiration towards
a good which he can only attain to by subjecting his
animal individuality to the law of reason.

Man does not know and cannot know any other
human life. Indeed, he only knows life in the
animal when the matter of which it is made is
subjected, not only to its own laws, but also to the
higher law of organism.

When there is in a certain combination of matter
submission to the higher law of organism, we recognize in this combination of matter life ; but when
this submission either has not begun or is ended,
and when we cannot see the line of demarcation
which separates this matter from the rest of matter
in which act only the laws of mechanics, chemistry,
and physics, then we do not recognize in it animal
life.

In this same way we only perceive life in our
fellows and in ourselves when our animal individuality is subject, not only to the law of organism,
but also to the higher law of the reasonable
consciousness.

As soon as there is no longer this submission of
the individuality to the law of reason, as soon as the
law of the individuality which governs the matter of
which man's body is composed is alone operative in
him, we can neither recognize nor perceive the
human life in others or in ourselves, just as we do
not see animal life in the matter which is only
governed by its own laws.

However energetic and rapid may be the movements of a man in delirium, in madness, in the

death-struggle, in drunkenness, in an outbreak of passion even, we do not recognize life in him, we do not treat him as a living man, we only admit that there is in him the possibility of life. But however weak and motionless a man may be, when we see that his animal individuality is in subjection to reason then we recognize life in him, and treat him accordingly.

We cannot understand human life in any other way than as the submission of the animal individuality to the law of reason.

This life is manifested in time and space but is not determined by the conditions of time and space; it is only determined by the degree of subjection of the animal individuality to reason. To judge of life by conditions of time and space is the same thing as to judge of the height of an object by its length and breadth.

The ascending movement of an object, which moves also in a horizontal plane, furnishes an exact image of the relationship between true human life and the life of the animal individuality, or between the true life and the life that is limited in space and time. The ascending movement of an object does not depend upon its horizontal movement, and can be neither increased nor lessened by it. It is the same with the determination of human life. True life is always manifested in the individuality, but is independent of it, and can be neither increased nor diminished by the one or other existence of individuality.

The conditions of time and space which determine the animal individuality of man can have no influence on the true life, which consists in the subjection of this animal individuality to the reasonable consciousness.

It is not in the power of a man who desires to live to suppress or to arrest the movement of his

existence in time and space, but his true life, that is
to say the attaining of welfare by submission to
reason, is independent of these visible movements
in time and space.

It is only in this progressive movement, with the
view of attaining to welfare by submission to reason,
that consists what constitutes human life. Without
this increase in submission, human life follows the
two visible directions of time and space, and is one
existence. When this ascending movement takes
place, that is to say this progressive submission to
reason, a relationship is established between two
forces on the one hand, and a third on the other
hand, and there is produced, following the resultant
of these forces, a movement greater or less, which
lifts the existence of man into the region of life.

The forces of time and space are defined, they are
bounded, they are incompatible with the idea of
life ; but the force of aspiration towards good by
submission to reason, is an ascending force : it is the
essential force of life, for which there are no limits
in time or space.

It seems to man that life stops and is divided, but
these stoppages and these pauses are only an error
of the consciousness (like the deception of the
external senses). True life can experience neither
stoppage nor pause ; we are but duped by our false
idea of life.

Man begins to live the true life, that is to say to
raise himself to a certain height above the animal
life, and from this height he perceives the phantom
of his animal existence which is inevitably terminated
by death ; he sees that his superficial existence is
bounded on all sides by abysses ; and, not understanding that this ascending movement is life itself,
he is afraid of that which he sees from above.
Instead of recognizing as his life this force which
raises him, and following the road which has opened

before him, he is frightened by what he has discovered from above, he comes down again and
crouches as low as possible, so that he may not see
the abysses he has discovered. But the force of the
reasonable consciousness raises him up anew, he sees
again, and, seized with fear, falls again to earth, in
order not to see. And this continues until at last
he recognizes that to escape from the fear this movement of life causes him, which draws him fatally, he
must understand that the movement in the horizontal
plane, that is to say his existence in time and space,
is not his life, but that his life only consists in the
ascending movement, and that it is only in the submission of his individuality to the law of reason that
there is the possibility of happiness and of life. He
must understand that he has wings which raise him
above the abyss, and that without them he would
never have been able to rise, and would never have
seen the abyss. He ought to trust himself to his
wings and to fly where they carry him.

It is simply want of faith that produces these
symptoms of faltering, which seem so strange at first,
this coming to a standstill of true life and this division
of the consciousness into two.

It is only to the man who takes for his life his
animal existence, limited by time and space, that it
seems that the reasonable consciousness is manifested
from time to time during his animal existence.
Contemplating thus the manifestation in himself of
the reasonable consciousness, man asks himself when
and in what conditions this reasonable consciousness
manifested itself in him? But however much man
may investigate his past, he never finds the periods
of the manifestation of the reasonable consciousness ;
it seems to him either that it has never existed, or that
it has always existed. If it seems to him that there
have been intervals between the manifestations of
this reasonable consciousness, that is solely because

he does not look upon the life of this reasonable consciousness as his own life.

Regarding his life as an animal existence, determined by the conditions of time and space, man wishes to measure with the same measure the awakening and the activity of the reasonable consciousness; he asks himself from what date, for how long, in what conditions he has been in possession of this reasonable consciousness. But these intervals between the awakening of the reasonable life exist only for him who understands his life as the life of the animal individuality. These intervals have no existence for the man who understands his life as what it truly is, that is to say the activity of the reasonable consciousness.

Reasonable life exists. There is no other. Intervals of one minute or of fifty thousand years are indifferent for it, because for it time does not exist.

The true life of man, that from which he learns to understand every other form of life, is the aspiration towards good, which can only be attained to by the submission of his individuality to the law of reason. But neither reason nor the degree of submission to reason can be determined by space and time. The true life of man is fulfilled outside of space and time.

CHAPTER XV

The renunciation of the well-being of the animal individuality
is the law of human life.

LIFE is an aspiration towards good; aspiration towards good is life. It is thus that the whole of humanity has understood, understands now, and always will understand life. Thus, the life of man is aspiration towards human good, and aspiration towards human good is human life. The multitude, the men who do not think, understand the well-being of man as the welfare of his animal individuality.

False science, excluding the idea of good from the definition of life, considers life as an animal existence, and therefore sees the good of life only in animal welfare. Thus science falls into the same mistake as the ignorant multitude.

In both cases the mistake arises from confusing the personality, the individuality, as science calls it, with the reasonable consciousness. The reasonable consciousness includes in itself the individuality. But individuality does not include in itself reasonable consciousness. Individuality is a property common to both the animal and the man, in so far as he is animal. The reasonable consciousness is a property only of man.

The animal may live only for his body, nothing prevents him from living thus. He satisfies the wants of his individuality, and without having the consciousness of it serves his kind; but he does not know that he is an individuality. The reasonable man cannot live only for his body. He cannot live thus, because, knowing that he is an individuality, and that other beings are also individualities like himself, he knows all that must result from the relationships of these individualities.

If man aspired only to the well-being of his individuality, if he loved only himself, his individuality, he would not know that other beings also love themselves (just as animals do not know it). But when he knows himself to be an individuality, pressing towards the same goal as all the individualities surrounding him, he can no longer aspire to this well-being which his reasonable consciousness considers to be an evil, and his life can no longer consist in the striving after individual well-being. Man imagines at times that his aspiration towards good has for object the satisfaction of the needs of his animal individuality. This mistake arises from his taking for the goal of the activity of his reasonable consciousness what he sees taking place in his animal. This error is like that of a man who should let himself be guided in his waking state by what he had seen in a dream. And, when this error is upheld by false doctrines, there is brought about in the man a confusion of the individuality with the reasonable consciousness.

The reasonable consciousness is always showing man that the satisfaction of the needs of his animal individuality cannot be his good, and consequently cannot be his life, and then this consciousness draws him irresistibly towards that good and therefore that life which are natural to him and which are not contained in his animal individuality.

People ordinarily think and say that to give up one's individual well-being is an act of heroism, and a meritorious action on the part of a man. Giving up one's individual welfare is neither a meritorious action nor an act of heroism, it is an inevitable condition of the life of man. When man comes to recognize himself as an individual distinct from the whole world, he also comes to see the other individualities distinct from all the world, and that link which unites them; he sees the illusion of his individual welfare and the one reality of the only good that can satisfy his reasonable consciousness.

For the animal, an activity which has not as its aim individual welfare, but which is diametrically opposed to this well-being, is a negation of life; for man it is just the contrary; it is the activity of man, directed to the attaining of the welfare of his individuality, which is a complete negation of human life.

The animal, having no reasonable consciousness to show him the misery and the finiteness of his existence, thinks of individual welfare and the propagation of the species resulting therefrom as the supreme aim of life. Whereas for man, individuality is only the point of existence whence he discovers the true good of his life, and this does not coincide with individual well-being.

For man, the consciousness of his individuality is not life, but the point where life commences, this life which consists in the progressive attainment of that good which is natural to him, independent of the good of the animal individuality.

According to current ideas, human life is the fraction of time from the birth to the death of his animal body. But this is not human life; it is only man's existence as an animal individuality. The truth is that human life is something which is manifested in the animal existence, just as organic life is something which is manifested only in the existence of matter.

Just at first man represents to himself the visible aim of his individuality to be that of his life. This aim is visible and so seems to him to be intelligible. But the aims which his reasonable consciousness points out to him appear incomprehensible because they are invisible.

To the man corrupted by the false doctrines of the age, the needs of the animal, which manifest themselves and are seen in himself and in others, seem simple and clear, whereas the new needs of his reasonable consciousness appear to be quite the reverse; the satisfaction of these needs, not coming about of itself, but necessary for him to obtain, seems to him something complicated and obscure.

It is as terrible and as painful for a man to renounce the visible representation of life and to yield to the invisible consciousness of it, as it would be terrible and painful for a child to be born if it were able to feel its birth—but it cannot be avoided, when it is evident that the visible representation of life leads to death, whilst the invisible consciousness alone gives life.

CHAPTER XVI

The animal individuality is the instrument of life.

No arguments whatever can hide from man this evident and indisputable truth, that his individual existence is something that constantly perishes, that hastens on to death, and that consequently life cannot be in his animal individuality.

Man cannot help seeing that the existence of his individuality, from birth and childhood to old age and death, is nothing else than a constant expenditure and a diminution of this animal individuality which is terminated by inevitable death. Thus the consciousness of his life in the individuality, which has within it the desire of growth and of the indestructibility of individuality, cannot be other than an incessant contradiction and suffering, cannot be other than evil, while the sole meaning of his life is an aspiration towards good.

Whatever may be the true good of man, he is forced to renounce the well-being of the animal individuality.

The renunciation of the well-being of the animal individuality is the law of human life. If this law is not carried out freely and shown in submission to the reasonable consciousness, it will be carried out by force in each man at the time of the carnal death of his animal, when, overcome by the weight of his sufferings, he desires only one thing : to be delivered from the cruel consciousness of his perishing individuality, and to pass into some other form of existence.

Entrance into life and human life itself are like what takes place when its master brings a horse out of the stable and harnesses it. On coming out of the stable, the horse, perceiving the light of day and scenting liberty, imagines that this liberty is life, but it is harnessed and moves off. It feels a weight behind it, and if it believes that its life consists in running about in freedom, it begins to kick, falls, and sometimes kills itself. If it does not kill itself two courses lie open before it : either it walks, draws the load, and finds that it is not too heavy, and that being driven, far from being a misery, is a pleasure ; or else it kicks itself free—and then its master takes it to the mill to grind ; fastens it to the wall by a halter ; the wheel turns beneath its feet, it will stay in one spot in darkness and suffering. In neither case are its forces expended in vain. It performs its task, and the law is fulfilled in it. The only difference is that in the one case it will work with joy, while in the other against its will and with torture.

" But what is the use of this individuality, the well-being of which I must renounce, I, a man, in order to attain life ? " say those who take animal existence for life.

Why has man received as his portion this consciousness of individuality, which is opposed to the manifestation of his true life ? One may answer this question by asking another like it, one that an animal might ask striving for its own ends, for the preservation of its own life and of the species.

" Wherefore," he might demand, " this matter and its laws,—mechanical, physical, chemical, and others, —against which I must struggle to attain my ends ? If my vocation," the animal might say, " consists in the accomplishment of the animal life, then wherefore all these obstacles which I have to surmount ? "

It is clear to us that all matter and its laws, against which the animal struggles and to which it submits for the existence of its animal individuality, are not obstacles, but means for the attainment of its ends. It is only by the elaboration of matter and by means of its laws that the animal lives. It is the same with the life of man. The animal individuality in which the man finds himself, and which he is called upon to subject to his reasonable consciousness, is not an obstacle but a means by which he attains the aim of well-being. The animal individuality is for man the instrument with which he works. The animal individuality is for man the spade given to the rational being to dig with, and, in digging, to blunt and sharpen, and wear out ; but not polish and carefully preserve. It is a talent given to him for increase, not for preservation. " And whosoever wishes to save his life shall lose it. And whosoever loses his life for my sake shall find it." In these words it is stated that we cannot save that which must perish and is ceaselessly perishing, but that it is solely in renouncing what perishes and must perish, that is to say, our animal individuality, that we obtain the true life which does not perish and cannot perish. It is said that our true life begins only when we cease to consider as life what has never been and cannot be for us life—our animal existence. It is said that he who will save the spade given him to procure food for supporting life, — having saved the spade will lose both the spade and the life.

CHAPTER XVII

Birth by the Spirit

" You must be born again," said Christ. This does not mean that someone has commanded man to be born, but that he is inevitably led to this. To have life, it is necessary to be born again into this existence by the reasonable consciousness.

The reasonable consciousness is given to man in order that he may place his life in that well-being which this consciousness discloses to him. He who finds his life in this well-being has life ; he who does not find his life in it but in the well-being of the animal individuality, deprives himself thereby even of life itself.

‾ This is the definition of life given by Christ.

Men who take for life their striving after individual well-being, hear these words, but do not understand them, nor can they understand them. It seems to them that such words are destitute of meaning, or of no great importance, and only indicate a certain sentimental and mystical state of mind, as they are pleased to call it, let loose upon them. They cannot understand the meaning of these words which explains a state inaccessible to them, just as a dry grain which has not yet germinated could not understand the state of a moist grain beginning to germinate. To the dry grain the sun which with its rays shines upon the germinating seed which is being born to life, is nothing more than an accident of no importance, just a little increase of warmth and light; but to the seed which is germinating it is the cause of its birth to life. It is the same with the men who have not yet arrived at the inner contradiction of the animal individuality and the reasonable consciousness ; to them the light of the sun of reason is only an accident of no importance ; sentimental and mystical words. The sun gives life to those only in whom germination has already commenced.

What is the manner, the cause, the date, the place of this germination not only in man, but in the animal and the plant, no one has ever been able to find out. Christ has said in speaking of the germination of this life in man that no one knows it, nor can know it.

How indeed could man know how life germinates in him ? The life is the light of men, the life is the life, the origin of all. In what way could man find out how it germinates ? For him, it is only some-

thing that does not live, which is manifested in time
and space, which germinates and perishes.   But the
true life *is*, therefore for man it can neither germinate
nor perish.

CHAPTER XVIII

The demands of the reasonable consciousness.

YES, the reasonable consciousness says to man,
unmistakably and irrefutably, that in the actual
organisation of the world, seen from the point of
view of his own individuality, there can be no well-
being for him, for his individuality. Life means
the desire to obtain his own well-being, and yet he
sees that this well-being is impossible. But, how
strange!   Notwithstanding that he sees, without
any doubt, that well-being is impossible for him,
nevertheless that which causes him to live is just
the desire for this impossible good—for this well-being
only for himself.
  A man whose reasonable consciousness is awakened
(just awakened), but has not yet subjected to its laws
the animal individuality, if he does not kill himself
lives only in the hope of realising this impossible
well-being.   The sole aim of his life and actions is
to obtain well-being for himself alone, that all men
and even every living creature should live and act
solely for *his* happiness, for *his* joys, so that *he* may
escape sufferings and death.
  How strange!   Although his own experience, his
observation of the life of all who surround him, as
well as reason, show to every man without a shadow
of doubt the impossibility of arriving at this result,
show him that it is impossible to oblige other living
beings to leave off loving themselves, to love him
alone; in spite of all this, every man's life consists

only in compelling other beings, by means of wealth, power, honours, glory, flattery, imposture, no matter what—in compelling other beings, to live not for themselves, but for him alone; to love not themselves, but him alone.

Men have done and do their utmost for this end, and they see at the same time that they are trying to do what is impossible. "My life is a striving after happiness," says man to himself. "I can obtain happiness only when all beings love me more than themselves; but all beings love only themselves, so that all I do to compel them to love me is useless. It is useless, and yet I can do nothing else."

Centuries pass: men have calculated the distance of the stars, determined their weight, discovered the substance of the sun and planets, but the question of knowing how to reconcile the demands of individual well-being with the life of the world, which excludes the possibility of this well-being, remains for the majority of mankind as insoluble as it was five thousand years ago.

The reasonable consciousness says to every man: "Yes, you can obtain well-being, but only on condition that all men love you more than themselves." And this same reasonable consciousness shows man that this is an impossibility, because all men love only themselves. Consequently the sole well-being revealed to man by his reasonable consciousness is hidden anew from him by this very consciousness.

Centuries pass, and the problem of the happiness of human life remains, for the majority of mankind, as inexplicable as ever. And yet the problem was solved long ago. And all who learn the answer to the problem are always astonished that they did not guess it themselves; they seem to have known it for long, but to have forgotten it. This enigma, which seemed so hopeless in the midst of the false doctrines of the age, offers of itself its own simple solution.

" Thou wishest that all should live for thee, that all should love thee more than themselves ? Thy wish can be fulfilled, but on one condition only : that all beings shall live for the well-being of others and love others more than themselves. Then only wilt thou and all beings be loved by all, and thou in their number wilt obtain thy desired well-being. If indeed well-being is possible to thee only when all beings love others more than themselves, then thou, a living being, must love others more than thyself."

Only on this condition are life and happiness possible for man ; only on this condition can all that poisons the life of man be destroyed : the strife of beings, the torment of sufferings, and the terror of death.

Why indeed is the happiness of individual exist-ence impossible ? In the first place, because of the strife of beings in the search for individual good ; in the second place, because of the illusion of pleasure, which produces waste of life, satiety, and suffering ; and, in the third place, because of death. But, in order that the impossibility of well-being might be destroyed and that it might become attainable to man, it is worth while to admit in thought that man can exchange the strife for the welfare of his individual being for the struggle for the welfare of other beings.

Regarding the world according to his own repre-sentation of life as the strife for individual well-being, man has seen in the world the senseless struggle of individuals occupied in destroying each other. But he has only to recognize as his life the strife for the happiness of others in order to see the world under quite another aspect : to see side by side with the incidental changes of fortune in the strife of beings, the ceaseless and mutual service which these same beings render each other, service without which the existence of the world is inconceivable.

As soon as one accepts this idea, all the previous irrational activity directed towards the unattainable happiness of the individuality gives place to another activity, conformable with the law of the world, but directed to the attainment of the greatest amount of happiness possible for oneself and for the whole world.

The second cause of the misery of individual life and of the impossibility for man to obtain happiness, is the illusiveness of the pleasures of the individuality, which wear out the life and lead to satiety and suffering. But, from the time that man recognizes his life to consist in striving after the happiness of others, the illusive thirst for pleasure disappears, and the vain, sorrowful activity directed to filling the bottomless cask of the animal individuality, gives place to an activity conformable to the laws of reason, an activity of which the aim is to sustain the life of other beings, an activity indispensable to his own happiness. The intensity of his individual suffering, which destroys the activity of his life, is replaced by a feeling of compassion for others, and this feeling calls forth an activity undeniably rich in results, and a source of joy.

The third cause of the misery of individual existence is the fear of death. Let man make the happiness of his life consist, not in the well-being of his animal individuality but in the happiness of other beings, and the scarecrow of death will disappear for ever from his view.

The terror of death comes only from the fear of losing, at the time of the bodily death, the happiness of life. Consequently, if man could place his happiness in that of other beings, that is to say love them more than himself, death would not seem to him to be the cessation of happiness and of life, as it is for him who lives but for himself. He who lives for others cannot represent death as the annihilation of happiness and of life, because the happiness and the life of other beings, far from being annihilated by the death of the man devoted to their service, are very often augmented and confirmed by the sacrifice of his life.

CHAPTER XIX

Confirmation of the demands of the reasonable consciousness.

" But this is not life ! " replies in its trouble the bewildered human reason ; " it is renunciation of life, it is suicide."

" I know nothing about that," says the reasonable consciousness ; " I know that such is the life of man ; he has not, nor can he have, any other. More than that, I know that this is life and welfare for man and for the whole world. According to my former conception of the world, my life and that of everything that has existence, was evil and nonsense ; but, regarded from this point of view, it appears as the realisation of reason, which is implanted in man. I know that the supreme welfare of the life of every being, a welfare which is capable of being infinitely increased, can only be obtained by the law of the devotion of each to all, and of all to each."

" But if this law can be admitted in theory, it cannot in practice," replies in its trouble the bewildered consciousness of man. " At this moment others do not love me more than themselves, therefore I cannot love them more than myself, or deprive myself of joys for them, or expose myself to suffering. I care little for the law of reason, I want pleasure for myself, I want deliverance from suffering. At present beings are engaged in struggling against each other; if I alone abstain from struggling, I shall be crushed by the others. Little matters it to me by what theoretical means the supreme welfare of all may be obtained,—I want my supreme and actual happiness now," says the false consciousness.

"I know nothing about that," replies the reasonable consciousness. "I only know that your so-called enjoyments can only be welfare to you on condition that you do not procure them yourself, but that they are given to you by others. If, on the contrary, you seize them yourself they can but produce satiety and suffering, as they actually are. You can only be relieved of actual suffering when others free you, not when you do it yourself,—as now, when from fear of imaginary pains, you put an end to your life.

"I know that individual life—that is to say this life in which it is necessary for all to love themselves, for me to love myself alone, and for me to be able to obtain the largest possible share of enjoyment and to be delivered from suffering and death—is the greatest and most incessant suffering. The more I love myself, the more I struggle against others, the more I shall be hated, the more ferociously will they struggle against me; the more I strive to guard myself from suffering, the more unhappy shall I become; the more I try to guard myself from death, the more terrible will it appear to me.

"I know that, in spite of all his efforts, man can never obtain welfare so long as he will not live in conformity to the law of his life. And the law of his life is not strife, but on the contrary a mutual exchange of services between all beings."

"But I know life only in my own individuality. It is impossible for me to place my life to the happiness of other beings."

"I know nothing about that," replies the reasonable consciousness. "I only know that my life and that of the world, which formerly seemed to me to be bitter folly, now appears to me as an intelligible whole, living and aspiring for one sole good, by means of submission to the one law of reason which I recognize in myself."

"But that is impossible to me!" says the bewildered animal reason. And yet, there is not a man who does not accomplish this impossible thing, and who does not find in it the best happiness of life.

It is impossible to recognize one's welfare to consist in that of other beings,—and yet there is not a man who does not know circumstances where the welfare of others outside of himself has become his own welfare. " It is impossible to consider happiness to consist in sorrow and suffering for others." And yet for man to yield himself to this feeling of compassion is enough to cause all individual enjoyment to cease to have any meaning in his eyes, and the whole energy of his life to be transformed into toil and suffering for the welfare of others, and for this suffering and toil to become happiness to him. " It is impossible to sacrifice one's life for the welfare of others." Yet as soon as a man knows this feeling, not only does he cease to see and to fear death, but it even appears to him to be the greatest blessing he can obtain.

The reasonable man cannot help seeing that by admitting in theory the possibility of exchanging for the aspiration towards personal welfare the welfare of other beings, his life, formerly unreasonable and unhappy, becomes reasonable and happy. He cannot help recognizing also that by supposing the same idea of life to be in other men and other beings, the life of the whole world, from unreasonable and cruel as it formerly appeared to be, becomes the highest rational welfare that man can desire; instead of being absurd and aimless as it was, it receives for him a reasonable meaning. The goal of the life of the universe appears to such a man as infinite progress towards the light, and the union of all the beings in the universe. This union is the very aim of life; thanks to it, first men, then all beings, submitting more and more to the law of reason, will comprehend what at present it is only given to man to comprehend, the truth that the happiness of life is not obtained by the aspiration of each being towards its individual happiness, but by the aspiration (in conformity with the law of reason) of every being for the happiness of all the others.

Nor is this all. In admitting merely the possibility of exchanging for the aspiration towards his own happiness the aspiration towards the happiness of all other beings, man cannot help seeing that it is just in progressively renouncing his own individuality, and removing the aim of his activity from self to others, that all the forward march of humanity and of the living beings most closely associated with man consists. History shows to man, in an unanswerable manner, that the movement of life in general does not consist in the revival and in the increase of the strife of beings, but on the contrary in the diminution of discord, in the weakening of strife, and that life only progresses when the world, submitting itself to reason, passes from discord and enmity to concord and union. Admitting this, he cannot help seeing that men who used to devour each other do so no longer; that those who used to massacre prisoners and their own children, no longer put them to death; that soldiers who glorified murder, cease to glory in it; that those who instituted slavery abolish it; that those who killed animals begin to tame them rather than kill them, to feed on their milk and eggs instead of on their flesh; indeed, that they are beginning to restrain the destruction of the vegetable kingdom. He sees that the best of his neighbours blame the search for pleasure and preach restraint; **he sees that the** greatest men, those whom posterity admires, set the example of sacrificing their lives for the welfare of others.   He sees that what he only admitted to the demands of reason, is actually accomplished in the world, is confirmed by the past life of humanity.

And this is not all : yet more powerfully and convincingly than reason and history, this same thing is pointed out to man from quite another source, from the aspiration of his heart, which draws him, as towards an immediate good, towards the same activity which his reason points out, and which is expressed in his heart by love.

CHAPTER XX

The demands of the individuality appear incompatible with those of the reasonable consciousness.

REASON, argument, history, inward feeling, every-thing, it would seem, convinces man of the correctness of this conception of life ; nevertheless man, educated in the doctrines of the world, imagines that the satisfaction of the needs of his reasonable consciousness and his feeling cannot be the law of life.

" What ! not struggle for individual happiness, not seek enjoyment, not fly from suffering, not fear death !   It is impossible, it is the renunciation of the very life itself.   How can I renounce my in-dividuality when I feel its demands, which my reason shows me to be legitimate?" say with conviction the civilized men of our age.

How remarkable ! working people, simple folk, those who cultivate their intelligence very little, scarcely ever put forward their personal aspirations, and always experience needs the very opposite of those of the individuality.   On the other hand, the complete negation of the needs of the reasonable consciousness,—above all, the refusal to recognize the legitimacy of these needs, and the defence of the rights of the individuality, are only met with among people who are rich, refined, and cultivated.

The man who is educated, effeminate, an idler, will always maintain that the individuality has inalienable rights. The hungry man will not trouble to prove that it is necessary for man to eat, for he is aware that everybody knows it, and that one can neither prove nor deny it: he is content to eat.

This is because the simple man, who is said to be without education, spends all his life in bodily toil, has not depraved his reason but has kept it in all its integrity and strength.

The man, on the contrary, who has spent all his life meditating not only on insignificant and futile matters, but on subjects which it is not natural to man to think about, this man, I say, has perverted his reason,—it is no longer free. It is occupied with things which are not natural to it, and dwells on the needs of the individuality, their development, their growth, and the means of gratifying them.

"But I am conscious of the needs of my individuality, they are therefore legitimate," say the so-called educated men, reared in the doctrines of the age.

And it would be impossible for them not to be aware of the needs of their individuality, for their whole life is directed to the imaginary increase of their individual welfare. They suppose welfare of the individuality to consist in the satisfaction of these wants. What they call individual needs are all those conditions of individual existence towards which their attention is directed. Reason being applied exclusively to them, these needs grow and multiply *ad infinitum*, and the gratification of these needs,

7

which multiply ceaselessly, hides **from men the** needs of their true life.

So-called Social Science takes as the basis of its investigations the study of the wants of man without taking into account one embarrassing circumstance for this science, which is that man may either have no wants at all, as he who commits suicide or permits himself to die of hunger, or may have an actually incalculable number of them.

There are as many needs in the existence of the man-animal, as there are phases in this existence ; and these phases are as numerous as the radii of a sphere. They are the needs of food, drink, air, exercise of all the muscles and nerves ; the needs of work, rest, play, family life ; the needs of science, art, religion, of their variety ; the needs of the child, the youth, the grown man, the old man ; of the young girl, the woman, the old woman ; the needs of the Chinaman, the Parisian, the Russian, the Laplander. These needs vary according to the habits of the races, their diseases, etc. One might spend one's life enumerating the possible forms of the wants of the individual existence of man, without succeeding in naming them all.

All conditions of existence may turn into needs, and the number of the conditions of existence is inexhaustible.

But what are called wants are only the conditions of which one is conscious.

As soon as one is conscious of these conditions, they lose their true meaning, taking on the exaggerated importance which reason when applied to them assigns,—and they hide from us the true life.

The needs, that is to say the conditions of the animal existence of man, may be likened to an immense number of little balls making up some kind of body. All these little balls are of equal size, each has its own distinct place, and they are not crushed so long as they do not expand any farther. In the same way all the needs of man are equal and have their appointed place and produce no painful sensation so long as they are unconscious.

But it is sufficient for any one of these little balls to begin to expand (and they can be expanded so that one will take up more room than all the others) for it to crush into the others and be itself crushed into by them. The same with the needs of life: consciousness has but to be directed on any one of these needs, and this need, become conscious, can take up the whole life of man and cause his whole being to suffer.

CHAPTER XXI

What is required is not renunciation of our individuality, but the subjugation of individuality to the reasonable consciousness.

YES, to say that man does not feel the needs of his reasonable consciousness, but only those of his individuality, is to say that the animal desires, in the growth of which we have employed all our intelligence, have taken possession of us, and have hidden from our sight the true human life. The evil weed of vices which have multiplied, has choked the germ of the true life.

And how could it be otherwise in our age, when those who are considered the teachers declare openly that the highest degree of individual perfection is a general development of the refined wants of. the individuality; that the well-being of the masses consists in having many wants and the power to satisfy them; that in fact the welfare of mankind lies in the satisfaction of their wants.

How could men, brought up in such a doctrine say otherwise than that they do not feel the wants

of the reasonable consciousness, but solely those of
the individuality? And how could they feel the
demands of reason, when their entire reason is
entirely consecrated to the increase of their im-
moderate desires? How could they give up their
desires when these desires have absorbed their whole
life?

" Renunciation of the individuality is impossible,"
they usually say, trying purposely to alter the meaning and the terms of the question, by substituting
for the idea of submission of the individuality to
the law of reason the idea of renunciation of the
individuality.

" It is contrary to nature," say they, "and therefore impossible." But it is not a question of renouncing the individuality. Individuality for a
reasonable man is the same as respiration or the
circulation of the blood to the animal individuality.
How can animal individuality renounce the circulation of blood? One cannot even speak of such a
thing. There can then be no question, for a
sensible man, of renouncing his individuality; for
the individuality is to a reasonable man as much an
indispensable condition of his life as the circulation
of the blood is to the animal.

The animal individuality cannot and does not
formulate any want. It is reason wrongly directed
which formulates these demands,—reason directed,
not to the guidance and the illumination of life, but
to the growth of the individual desires.

The needs of the animal individuality can always
be satisfied. Man has not the right to say " What
shall I eat, or how shall I be clothed?" If he lives
the rational life all these wants are provided for, as
are those of the bird and the flower. And, indeed,
what thinking man can believe that he can diminish
the misery of his existence by protecting his individuality against want?

The misery of man's existence does not arise from his existence as an individuality, but from his considering the existence of this individuality as life and happiness. Only then appear the contradiction, the division, and the suffering of man.

Man's sufferings begin only when he employs the powers of his reason to strengthen and increase without end the growing needs of his individuality, so as to hide from himself the requirements of his reason.

Man neither can nor ought to renounce his own individuality any more than any other of all the conditions of his existence ; but neither can he nor ought he to take these conditions for life itself. One can and ought to make use of the present conditions of life, but one neither can nor ought to look on these conditions as the aim of life. Not to renounce the individuality but to renounce the happiness of the individuality, and to cease to consider it as life itself,—this is what man should do in order to return to unity, and that the happiness to which his life should aspire may be obtainable.

The great teachers of humanity have taught from the most remote times that to place one's life in the individuality is the annihilation of life, and that the only possible way of attaining to life is to renounce individual welfare.

Yes, but what is this ? "This is Buddhism !" it is usual for the men of our age to reply. "It is Nirvana, it is to stand on a pillar !" And when they have said this these men imagine they have triumphantly refuted what everyone knows very well, what we can disguise from no one : the knowledge that individual life is miserable and entirely devoid of meaning.

"It is Buddhism, Nirvana," say they, and they think they have refuted by these words what has been admitted and still is believed by thousands of millions of men, what each of us knows perfectly in his inmost soul, namely, that life dedicated to the pursuit of individual ends is fatal and senseless, and that if there is any escape whatever from this perdition and this nonsense it can only be by the renunciation of the welfare of the individuality.

They are not at all troubled that the great majority of humanity have understood and do understand life thus, that the greatest minds have understood it in the same way, and that no one could understand it any other way. They are so fully convinced that all the problems of life, when not solved in the most pleasing manner, may be evaded, thanks to the telephone, operettas, bacteriology, electric light, and so on, that the idea of the renunciation of the welfare of individual life seems to them to be nothing else than a remnant of ancient ignorance.

And yet these unhappy people never suspect that the crudest Hindoo, who stands for years on one foot in the name of the renunciation of individual well-being in order to reach Nirvana, is incomparably more alive than they are, these representatives of our contemporary European society, returned to the condition of animals, running over the earth on iron rails, and showing to the whole world their animalism by the light of electricity. This Hindoo has grasped the fact that there is contradiction between the life of the individuality and the reasonable life, and he solves it after his own fashion ; the men of our civilised world not only have not understood this contradiction, but do not even believe that it exists.

The proposition that human life is not individual existence, this truth, won at the cost of the moral toil of humanity during thousands of years, has become for the non-animal man in the moral kingdom a truth, not only of the same importance as the rotation of the earth and the laws of gravitation, but even far more unquestionable and more invincible. Every thinking man, scholar, ignoramus, old man, child, all understand and recognise this ; it is hid only from the most savage natives of Africa and Australia, and from the men who live in the towns and capitals of Europe secure against want and have returned to savagery. This truth has become the patrimony of humanity, and if humanity does not retrograde in its accessory knowledge, in mechanics, algebra, astronomy, still less can it retrograde in the fundamental and principal science, whose object is to define life. It is impossible to forget and obliterate from the consciousness of humanity what it has gained during its life of several thousand years, that is to say, the conviction of the vanity, the meaninglessness, and the misery of individual existence. The attempts made to revive the antediluvian and savage idea of life regarded as individual existence—attempts which occupy the so-called science of our European world—only show in a more conclusive manner the growth of the reasonable consciousness in humanity, and indicate clearly at what point humanity shook off its swaddling clothes. The philosophical theories of self-destruction and their practical application, revealed by the alarming extent to which suicide has increased, show the impossibility of man returning to the degree of consciousness already lived through.

Humanity has finished with the idea of life considered as individual existence ; it cannot return to it, and it is impossible to forget that the individual existence of man has no meaning. However much we have written, spoken, discovered, perfected our individual life, the denial of the possibility of individual welfare remains an immovable truth for all rational men in our age.

"And yet, it moves!" Our business is not to refute the theories of Galileo and Copernicus, nor

to invent new Ptolemaic Circles—an impossibility,
—but our business is to go further, to draw the
extreme deductions from the proposition already
admitted by the general consciousness of humanity.
Just so with the proposition of the impossibility of
individual happiness which is recognized equally by
the Brahmins, by Buddha, Lao-Tsi, Solomon, the
Stoics, and all the true thinkers of humanity.   We
must not conceal from ourselves this idea, nor try to
elude it in any possible way; we must admit it
frankly and courageously, and draw from it its most
extreme deductions.

CHAPTER XXII

The feeling of love is the manifestation of the activity of the
individuality subjected to the reasonable consciousness.

A REASONABLE being cannot devote his life to the
pursuit of the aims of the individuality.   He cannot,
because all roads are closed to him, and the aims
towards which the animal individuality of man tends
is evidently inaccessible.   The reasonable consciousness reveals to him other aims, which are not only
within his reach, but fully satisfy his reasonable consciousness.   Nevertheless, at first sight, under the
influence of the false doctrine of the world, man
imagines that these aims are in contradiction to his
individuality.
However much a man, brought up in our time,
the appetites of whose individuality are developed
to an extreme, may strive to recognize himself in his
reasonable I, he does not feel in that I the longing
for life which he feels in his animal individuality.
It appears that the reasonable I only contemplates
life, but does not itself live, and has no longing for
life.   The reasonable I feels no longing for life, and

the animal self is obliged to suffer; consequently, there is nothing to be done but to rid oneself of life.

It is in this unconscientious way that the negative philosophers of our time (Schopenhauer and Hartmann) solve the problem: they deny life while remaining in it, instead of availing themselves of the possibility of going out of it.

And it is thus that those who commit suicide solve in good faith this question: by quitting life where they see nothing but evil for themselves.

Suicide appears to them the only way of escaping the absurdity of human life in the present day.

The argument of the pessimistic philosophy and of the greater number of those who commit suicide is as follows: "There is an animal *I*, which longs for life. This *I*, with its longing, cannot be satisfied. There is another, a reasonable *I*, which has no longing for life, which contents itself with critically contemplating all the false joy of living and the passions of the animal self, and renounces them entirely.

"If I give myself up to the first self, I see that I live in an unreasonable manner, that I am going to misery, in which I plunge more and more profoundly. If I give myself up to the second, to the reasonable *I*, it leaves me without desire of life. I see that it is absurd and impossible to live only to obtain what I want, that is to say the welfare of my individuality. One could perhaps live for the reasonable consciousness, but it is useless, and not worth the trouble. Serve the principle whence I have come — God. Why? God, if He exists, has quite enough servants without me; why should I serve Him?

"One may contemplate all this game of life so long as it is not wearisome; as soon as it is wearisome, one can go away. kill oneself. That is what I will do."

Such is the contradictory conception of life to which humanity had arrived before Solomon, before

Buddha, and to which the false teachers of our age would bring us back.

The wants of the individuality are carried to the extreme limits of absurdity. The awakened reason disowns them. But the individual wants are so increased, they have so invaded the consciousness of man, that it seems to him as if reason renounces life entirely.

He imagines that in excluding from his consciousness of life all that his reason renounces, nothing will remain. He cannot yet see what remains. That remainder, which contains all life, appears to him void.-

" But the light shineth in the darkness, and the darkness cannot comprehend it."

The doctrine of the truth places man in this dilemma : either he must live an absurd existence, or renounce this life ; and it gives him the solution.

The doctrine, which is always called the doctrine of good, the doctrine of truth, has taught men that in place of this delusive good which they seek for the animal individuality, they can obtain immediately, in the very place they happen to be, and not at some unknown time or place, the real good, imprescriptible, which is always within reach.

This good is not the mere deduction of an argument ; it is not something for which one must seek somewhere ; it is not a good promised at some unknown place and time; but it is the good that man knows the best, and towards which is immediately drawn every uncorrupted human soul.

All men know, from the very earliest years of childhood, that besides the good of the animal individuality, there exists a superior good in life, which is not only independent of the satisfying of the appetites of the animal individuality ; but, on the contrary, becomes greater, the greater the renunciation of the welfare of the animal individuality.

All men know the feeling which solves all the
contradictions of human life and gives supreme welfare to man; this feeling is *love*.

Life is the activity of the animal individuality,
subjected to the law of reason. Reason is that law
to which the animal individuality of the man must
be subjected in order to obtain welfare. Love is
the only reasonable activity of man.

The animal individuality longs for its good; reason
shows man the illusion of individual good and leaves
him but one path. Activity in this path is love.

The animal individuality of man demands happiness; the reasonable consciousness shows him the
misery of all the beings occupied in struggling with
each other; it shows him that welfare is inaccessible
to his animal individuality, that the only good which
could be within his reach would be that which would
not cause strife with other beings, nor cessation of
welfare, nor satiety, nor the vision and horror of
death.

And behold! man discovers in his soul a feeling
which is as a key that fits only this lock. This
sentiment gives him the very welfare which his
reason indicates as being the only possible one.
And this feeling not only solves the preceding contradiction of life, but even finds, so to speak, in this
very contradiction the possibility of manifesting itself.
The animal individualities endeavour in order to
obtain their objects to make use of the individuality
of man for themselves; and the feeling of love causes
man to devote his existence to the use of other
beings.

The animal individuality suffers. And it is precisely
these sufferings and their relief which form the
principal object of the activity of love. In aiming
at welfare the animal individuality with every breath
rushes towards the supreme evil, death, the vision of
which disturbs all individual pleasure; but the feeling

of love not only causes that terror to disappear, but
inclines man even to the extreme sacrifice of his
carnal existence for the welfare of others.

CHAPTER XXIII

The manifestation of the feeling of love is impossible to men
who do not understand the meaning of their life.

EVERY man knows that in the feeling of love there is
something special, capable of solving all the contradictions of life and of giving to man that complete
welfare, the striving after which constitutes his life.
" But it is a feeling that comes but rarely, lasts only a
little while, and is followed by still worse sufferings,"
say the men who do not understand life.

To these men love appears not as the sole and
legitimate manifestation of life, as the reasonable
consciousness conceives it to be, but only as one of
the thousand different eventualities of life ; as one of
the thousand varied phases through which man passes
during his existence. Sometimes he is a dandy,
sometimes he applies himself to science or art, sometimes to his functions, sometimes he allows himself
to be absorbed by ambition, by the desire of gain,
sometimes he loves someone. The state of love
appears to men who do not understand life, not as
the very essence of human life, but as an accidental
condition, as independent of his will as all others
through which he passes during his life. It even
happens often that he reads and hears opinions that
love is something abnormal which deranges the
regular course of life—a state of torture, something
similar to what must happen to the owl when the
sun rises. ·

They feel, it is true, that in the state of love there
is something special, something more important, than

in all the other states. But, as they do not understand life they cannot understand love, and thus the
state of love seems to them as miserable and deceptive
as all the other states.

"Love? . . . But whom, then? For a little
while it is not worth while, and to love for ever is
impossible."

These words express exactly the confused knowledge of men that in love there is the remedy for
all the miseries of life,—the unique something which
resembles true welfare ;—and yet the avowal that
love cannot be the anchor of salvation for men who
do not understand life. Love no one, and love goes.
Consequently love is a welfare only when there is
someone to love, and someone whom it is possible to
love for ever. But as this is not possible, there is no
salvation in love, and love is a deception and a suffering like all the rest.

They could not understand love in any other way,
these men who teach and who have themselves
learned that life is nothing else than animal existence.
For such people love does not answer to the idea
which we involuntarily attach to the word. It is not
a beneficent activity which gives welfare to those
who love and for those who are loved. In the ideas
of men who recognize life in animal individuality,
love is often the feeling in consequence of which one
mother, for the welfare of her infant, deprives another
hungry child of its mother's milk, and suffers from
anxiety for the success of the nursing ; the feeling
which drives a father at the cost of great pain to take
away the last morsel of bread from famishing people
to assure the existence of his own children ; the
feeling which causes the man who loves a woman to
suffer from that love and to make her suffer, by
seducing her, through jealousy, or destroys himself
and her ; the feeling by which it even happens that
a man violates a woman ; the feeling which makes

the men of one association do harm to others in order to safeguard the interests of their associates ; the same feeling by which a man worries himself over a favourite occupation, and with this occupation causes affliction to all who surround him ; under the influence of this feeling men, unable to endure an affront offered to a beloved country, cover the battle-fields with killed and wounded friends and enemies.

Further, for men who understand life to consist in the welfare of the animal individuality, the activity of love offers such difficulties that its manifestations become not only painful, but often impossible. " One should not reason about love," those men usually say who do not understand life, " but abandon oneself to the immediate feeling of preference and partiality which one experiences for men: that is the true love."

They are right in saying that one should not reason about love, and that all reasoning about love destroys it. But the point is, that only those people need not reason about love who have already used their reason to understand life and who have renounced the welfare of the individual existence ; but those who have not understood life and who exist for the welfare of the animal individuality, cannot help reasoning about it. They must reason to be enabled to give themselves up to this feeling which they call love.

Every manifestation of this feeling is impossible for them, without reasoning, and without solving unsolvable questions.

In reality every man prefers his own child, his wife, his friends, his country, to the children, wives, friends, and country of others, and he calls this feeling love. To love means in general to do good. It is thus that we all understand love, and we do not know how to comprehend it in any other way. Thus, when I love my child, my wife, my country, I mean that I desire the welfare of my child, wife, country more than that of other children, women, and countries. It never happens, and can never happen, that I love my child, wife, or country only. Every man loves at the same time his child, wife, country, and men in general. Nevertheless the conditions of the welfare which he desires for the different beings loved, in virtue of his love, are so intimately connected, that every activity of love for one of the beings loved not only hinders his activity for the others but is detrimental to them.

And therefore the following questions arise: In the name of which love should I act and how should I act? In the name of which love should I sacrifice another love? Whom shall I love the most and to whom do the most good—to my wife, or to my children ;—to my wife and children, or to my friends? How shall I serve a beloved country without doing injury to the love for my wife, children, and friends?

Finally, how shall I solve the problem of knowing in what measure I can sacrifice my individuality, which is necessary to the service of others? To what extent can I occupy myself with my own affairs and yet be able to serve those I love?

All these questions seem very simple to people who have not tried to explain this feeling they call love, — but, far from being simple, they are quite unsolvable.

It was not without purpose that the lawyer put the question to Christ, "Who is my neighbour?" The answer to such questions seems very easy only to men who forget the real conditions of human life.

If men were gods, as we imagine, then it might be possible for them to love only the men of their choice ; only then could the act of preferring one to another be true love. But men are not gods. They find themselves in conditions of existence whereby all living beings live always each one at the expense of others, devouring each other literally or figuratively ; and man, in so far as he is a reasonable being, must know and see this. He must know that every material welfare is obtained by one being only at the expense of another. However much men believe the religious and scientific superstitions about a future golden age in which everyone shall have enough, the reasonable man sees and knows that the law of his existence in time and space is the struggle of all against each, and of each against all.

In the press and struggle of animal interests which make up the life of the world it is impossible for man to love some chosen ones, as men imagine who do not understand life. Even if man does love some chosen ones, he never loves one only. Every man loves his mother, and wife, and child, and friends, and country, and even all people. And love is not only a word (as all are agreed in this), but it is an activity directed to the welfare of others. But this activity does not express itself in a settled order, the demands of the strongest love appearing first, those of a feebler love second, and so on. The demands of love present themselves all together incessantly and without any order. Here is a starving old man for whom I have a little love, who comes to ask of me the food I have reserved for the supper of my much loved children; how shall I decide between the present demand of a feebler love and the future demand of a stronger one?

These questions are the same as the one put by the lawyer to Christ, " Who is my neighbour? "

In fact, how am I to decide whom it is necessary to serve, and to what extent?—Men, or the mother-country? The country or my friends? My friends or my wife? My wife or my father? My father or my children? My children or myself (in order that I may be in a position to devote myself to the service of others when necessary)?

The demands of love are so many, and they are all so closely interwoven, that the satisfaction of the demands of some deprives man of the possibility of satisfying others. But if I admit that I cannot clothe a child benumbed with cold, on the pretence that my children will one day need the clothes asked of me, I can also resist other demands of love in the name of my future children.

It is the same in relation to love for my country, for my favourite occupations, and for humanity. If a man is capable of resisting the demands of a feeble love which is present, in the name of the demands of a greater love yet to come, then it is evident that such a man will never be able, even when he wishes it with all his might, to decide in what measure he can renounce the demands of the present in the name of the future ; consequently, not being in a position to decide this question, he will choose always the manifestations of love which please him —in other words, he will act not in the name of love, but in the name of his individuality. If a man decides that it is better for him to resist the demands of a present feeble love, in the name of another, of a future manifestation, he deceives either himself or other people, and loves no one but himself.

Future love does not exist. Love is a present activity only. The man who does not manifest love in the present has not love.

The same thing happens with the idea of life of the men who have not life. If men were animals merely, if they were devoid of reason, they would lead the existence of animals and would not reason about life ; their animal existence would be lawful and happy. It is the same with respect to love ; if men were animals merely, devoid of reason, they would love those things that animals love : their cubs, their herds, and would not know that they loved their cubs and herds ; neither would they know that wolves love their cubs and that members of other herds love their companions ; in a word, their love

8

and their life would be that love and that life natural to that degree of consciousness in which they exist.

But men are reasonable beings, and must necessarily see that other beings have a similar love for those near them, and consequently that these feelings of love must come into collision, and produce something not good but entirely contrary to the idea of love.

But if men make use of their reason to justify and strengthen this bad, animal feeling which they call love, giving it monstrous proportions, then the feeling becomes not only not good, but makes man (a truth known for a long time) the most wicked and terrible animal. Then happens what is spoken of in the Gospels.

" If the light that is in you be darkness, how great is that darkness." If there were in man nothing but his love for himself and for his children, there would not be a ninety-ninth part of the evil there is now amongst men. Ninety-nine parts of the evil amongst men arise from that false feeling which they, praising it, call love, and which no more resembles love than the life of the animal resembles the life of the man.

This, which men, not understanding life, call love, simply consists in the preference for certain conditions of their individual welfare to other conditions. When a man, who does not understand life, says that he loves his wife, or child, or friend, he merely expresses the fact that the presence in his life of his wife, child, and friend, adds to the welfare of his individual life.

These preferences bear the same relation to love as existence bears to life. As men who do not understand life give this name to existence, so these men use the word love for preferring certain conditions of individual existence to other conditions.

This feeling, that is to say these preferences for certain beings, as, for example, for one's own children, or even for certain occupations, such as science or art, we also call love; it is such feelings, such preferences infinitely varied, that constitute all the complexity of the visible and palpable animal life of men; they cannot be called love, because they do not possess the chief characteristic of love : activity, which has for object and result—welfare.

The passion with which these preferences are manifested only shows the energy of the animal individuality. The passion improperly called love, which makes us prefer certain men to others, is but a wild tree on which the true love can be grafted and may produce fruit. But just as the wild stock is not an apple-tree and does not bear fruit, or bears only bitter fruit instead of sweet, so partiality is not love, and does not do good to men, nay, even it may do great human evil. And therefore it brings the greatest evil in the world, this love so praised, for wife, for children, for friends, not to speak of love for science, art, and one's country, which is no other than the preference for a time of certain conditions of animal life to others.

CHAPTER XXIV

True love is a consequence of the renunciation of the welfare of the individuality.

TRUE love becomes possible only when one renounces the welfare of the animal individuality.

The possibility of true love begins only when man has understood that it is not for the welfare of his animal individuality; only when all the sap of his life passes into the noble graft of true love, growing with all the vigour of the trunk of this wild tree, the animal individuality. The doctrine of Christ is the graft of this love, as he said himself. He said that he himself, his love, is the one vine-stock which bears fruit, and that every branch which does not bear fruit is cut off.

True love is only intelligible to him who has not only understood, but has recognized in his life the truth of these words : " Whosoever would save his life shall lose it, but whosoever shall lose his life for my sake shall save it."

Only he who has understood that " whoso hateth his life in this world shall save it in the life eternal," knows true love.

" He who loveth father or mother more than me is not worthy of me. He who loveth son or daughter more than me is not worthy of me." " For if you love only those who love you, it is not love : love your enemies, love those who hate you."

It is not in consequence of love for father, son, wife, friends, for those who are good and amiable, as people ordinarily think, that men renounce the individuality, it is simply as a consequence of the consciousness of the vanity of individual existence, of the consciousness of the impossibility of welfare for that existence ; therefore it is only in renouncing individual life that man comes to the knowledge of true love, and can truly love his father, son, wife, children, and friends.

Love is the preferring other beings before ourselves,—before our animal individuality.

The neglect of the immediate interests of the individuality with the object of attaining the distant aims of the same individuality, occurring with the so-called love which has not grown to self-abnegation, is nothing but the action of preferring certain beings to others with the object of obtaining individual welfare.

True love, before it becomes an active feeling,

must exist as a certain condition. The principle of love, its root, is not, as people usually think, an outburst of feeling which obscures reason; it is, on the contrary, a most rational, luminous, and therefore calm and joyous condition, peculiar to children and rational people.

This condition is a state of benevolence towards all men which is natural to the child, but which in a grown man arises only by renunciation, and grows only in proportion to the renunciation of the welfare of the individuality.

How often we hear it said, " It is all the same to me, I do not want anything "; and we see at once that those who speak in this way are animated by ill-will to others. But let each man try at least once, in a moment of ill-will to men, to say to himself sincerely from his soul : " It is all the same to me ; I do not want anything "; let him strive, be it but for an instant, to renounce every individual desire, and every man will see by this simple inner experiment with what rapidity and in proportion to the sincerity of his renunciation all ill-will will disappear, and how afterwards what benevolence towards all men will well forth from his heart, closed until now.

Indeed, love is the preference of other beings to oneself; it is thus that we understand love, and we could not understand it otherwise. The magnitude of love is the magnitude of a fraction of which the numerator—my partialities, my sympathies for others —does not depend upon me ; whilst the denominator —my love for myself—can be increased or decreased by me to any extent, according to the importance I attach to my animal individuality. The arguments of the world about love and the extent of it are arguments on the magnitude of the fractions according to the numerators only, without taking any account of the denominators.

True love has always as its basis the renunciation

of individual welfare and the feeling of benevolence
for others which results therefrom.   True love for
certain men, relations or strangers, can only grow in
this general benevolence.   It is only such love
which can give the true welfare of life and solve
the apparent contradiction between the animal and
reasonable consciousness.   Love which does not rest
upon the renunciation of the individuality and, its
consequence, on the benevolence towards all men,
is nothing but animal life ; and this life is exposed
to the same and to yet greater ills and yet greater
unreasonableness than life without this pretended
love.

The feeling of partiality which is called love, not
only does not do away with the struggle for existence,
does not free the individuality from the pursuit of
pleasures, does not deliver from death, but really
darkens life yet more, renders the struggle more
furious, increases the thirst for pleasures for oneself
and for others, and augments the fear of death for
oneself and for them.

He who understands life to consist in the existence of the animal individuality cannot love,
because love must appear to him an activity
diametrically opposed to his life.   The life of such
a man lies solely in the welfare of the animal existence, and love demands before everything . the
sacrifice of this welfare.   If one who does not understand life sincerely desired to apply himself to the
activity of love he would be unable to do so until he
had comprehended life and modified altogether his
relations to it.

He who places his life in the welfare of the animal
individuality employs all his time in increasing the
resources of his animal welfare, in acquiring riches
and preserving them ; he obliges others to contribute
to his animal welfare, and distributes his favours to
those who have done most to ensure the welfare of

his individuality. How could he make the sacrifice of his life when it is supported not by himself, but by others? It is yet more difficult for him to choose, among the men whom he prefers, one to whom he will transmit the goods which he has accumulated, and whom to serve.

In order to be able to give his life, he must at the very first renounce that surplus which he has made out of others for the welfare of his life; he ought then to do an impossibility: decide as to which of his fellow-creatures he ought to devote his life. But before he can love, that is to say sacrifice himself to do good, he must cease from hatred, that is, from doing evil; he must cease from preferring some people to others for the welfare of his individuality.

Active love, which alone can satisfy the man and his fellow-creatures, is only possible to one who does not place welfare in the individual life, consequently is not absorbed in this false welfare, but allows free action to the feeling of benevolence for others which is natural to man.

The welfare of the life of such a man is in love, as that of the plant is in light, and therefore as the uncovered plant cannot ask and does not ask anything as to which side to grow, whether the light is good, and whether it must not wait for another better light, but takes the sole light which is diffused over the world, and stretches towards it,—so the man who has renounced the welfare of his individuality does not reason about what he ought to restore of what he has taken from other men, and to which beloved beings; and whether there is not some still better love than that which makes demands upon him; but he gives himself up entirely and devotes his existence to the love that is within his reach and which he sees before him. Only such love gives complete satisfaction to the reasonable nature of man.

CHAPTER XXV

Love is the sole and complete activity of the true life.

THERE is no other love than that which consists in giving one's life for one's friend. Love is only really love when it is a sacrifice of self. Only when a man gives to another not only his time and his strength, but wears out his body for the object loved, giving him his life, then alone do we all recognize that this is love, and only in such love we all find happiness —the recompense of love. And it is only because there is such love in men that this world exists.

A mother who suckles her children gives herself directly, gives her own body to nourish the children, who are unable to live without it. This is love. So, the workman, who for the welfare of others, wears out his body by toil, and thus brings himself to the verge of death, also gives himself, his body, to nourish others. And such love is possible only to the man for whom, between the possibility of the sacrifice of himself and those beings whom he loves, no obstacle to sacrifice exists. The mother who trusts her child to a foster-mother cannot love it; the man occupied in acquiring and keeping riches cannot love.

" He that saith he is in the light, and hateth his brother, is in the darkness even until now. He that loveth his brother abideth in the light, and there is none occasion of stumbling in him. But he that hateth his brother is in the darkness, and walketh in the darkness, and knoweth not whither he goeth, because the darkness hath blinded his eyes. . . . Let us not love in word, neither with the tongue; but in deed and truth. Hereby shall we know that we are of the truth, and shall assure our heart before him. . . . Herein is love made perfect with us, that we may have boldness in the day of judgment; because as he is, even so (we may be) in this world. There is no fear in love ; but perfect love casteth out fear, because fear hath punishment ; and he that feareth is not made perfect in love."

Only such love gives true life to men.

" Thou shalt love the Lord thy God with all thy heart and with ·all thy soul and with all thy mind. This is the first and the greatest commandment."

The second is like unto it.　" Thou shalt love thy neighbour as thyself," said the lawyer to Christ.　To this Jesus replied : " Thou hast answered rightly ; do this, *i.e.* love God and thy neighbour, and thou *shalt live.*"

True love is life itself.　" We know by this that we have passed from death unto life," because we love our brothers, said the disciple of Christ.　" He that loveth not his brother abideth in death."　He only lives, who loves.

Love, according to the doctrine of Christ, is life itself, not a life unreasonable, suffering, perishable, but a life happy and eternal.　And we know this.

Love is not the deduction of reason, is not the result of a certain activity ; but it is the most joyous activity of the life which surrounds us on all sides, and which we have all felt in us from the first memories of our infancy up to the moment when the false doctrines of the world stifled it in our souls and rendered us incapable of experiencing it.

Love is not a preference for what adds to the temporary welfare of the individuality of man, like love for chosen beings or objects, but it is the longing for the welfare of others which remains in man after he has renounced the welfare of his animal individuality.

Where is the living man who does not know this feeling of bliss by having experienced it at least once, and most frequently in his early childhood before his soul was obstructed by all the deceitful doctrines which stifle life in us,—this feeling of happiness and gentleness which makes us wish to love all neighbours, father, mother, brothers, bad people and enemies, and the dog and the horse and the blade of grass; which makes us desire but one thing—that it should be well with all, that all should be happy, and still more desire to act so that it would be well with all? To sacrifice ourselves and our whole life in order that all may be happy and contented is alone love, and in this only is the life of man.

This love, in which alone is life, manifests itself in the human soul like a tender shoot hardly noticeable among the coarse shoots of the rough grasses which resemble it, those various appetites of man which we call love. At first, to people and to the man himself, it seems that this shoot, whence will grow the tree where the birds must find shelter, resembles all the other shoots. Men even prefer at first the shoots of the coarse weeds which grow more rapidly, and the one shoot of life is stifled and decays. But what is more grievous, and what happens more frequently, is that men, having heard that among these shoots there is one called love, the only true one, the only one capable of giving life, set themselves to cultivate another shoot of the coarse weeds, which they call by the same name, love, and in doing so trample under foot the only true one. But what is still worse, men seize with brutal hand the shoot itself and cry: "Here it is, we have found it. We know it now, let us cultivate it. Love! Love! This is the sublime feeling, here it is." And they begin to transplant it, to try to improve it; and the shoot, because it is handled and bruised, dies before it has flowered; and then these men or their friends, say, "This is all absurdity, folly, sentimentality." The shoot of love, so tender at its appearance, sensitive to all touch, becomes strong only when fully developed. All that men do to it only makes it worse. All it needs is, that nothing should hide from it the sun of reason, which alone makes it grow.

CHAPTER XXVI

The efforts of men, directed to the impossible amelioration of their existence, deprive them of the possibility of living the one true life.

ONLY the recognition of the phantasy and illusion of the animal existence and the emancipation in himself of the one true life of love gives man welfare. And what then shall men do to obtain this welfare? Those whose existence is nothing else than a slow destruction of the individuality and a march towards the inevitable death of that individuality, which they cannot ignore, these men have no other aim during their existence, and make no efforts for anything else, than to sustain this individuality which perishes and to satisfy its appetites, depriving themselves of the possibility of the only welfare of life—love.

The activity of these men, who do not understand life, is employed during their whole existence in struggling for this existence, in procuring pleasure, avoiding suffering, and warding off that death which they cannot escape.

But the interest of pleasures increases also the violent intensity of the struggle, the faculty of feeling the pain, and the advancing nearness, of death. There is only one way to hide the approach of death: to continually increase pleasure. But the increase of pleasure reaches its limits; and pleasure incapable of being increased changes into pain, and there remains only the faculty of feeling pain more keenly and the horror of that death which steadily approaches in the midst of the pain. A "vicious circle" appears : one thing is the cause of the other, and that one augments the other. The great misfortune of the life of men who do not understand life is that the things they consider as pleasures (all the enjoyments of the life of riches) are of such a nature that they cannot be distributed equally among all, but must be taken from others and obtained by violence, by evil, by destroying the possibility of that benevolence towards others out of which grows love. So that pleasures are always diametrically opposed to love, and the stronger they are, the more they are opposed to it. Consequently the stronger and more intense the activity for the attainment of pleasures, the more impossible becomes the sole welfare accessible to man, which is love.

Life is understood not as the reasonable consciousness conceives it to be, as an invisible, but undisputed, submission of the animal to the law of reason, an incessant submission which sets free that benevolence towards all others which is natural to man, and the activity of love which results from it ; but life is only regarded as a temporary carnal existence, in conditions decided upon and established by us, which, on the contrary, exclude the possibility of benevolence to all.

To men imbued with the doctrine of the age, who have employed their reason to establish certain conditions of existence, it appears that the increase of the welfare of life proceeds from a better external arrangement of one's existence. But a better external arrangement of their existence depends upon an increase of the violence practised upon other men, which is diametrically opposed to love. So that the better their arrangement, the less possibility there remains to them of love—of life.

Never having employed their reason to understand

that the welfare of the animal existence of all men without exception is nothing, is a cipher, they have taken this cipher for a quantity capable of being diminished and augmented, and they devote to this sham augmentation, to the multiplication of the cipher, all their unapplied reason.

Men do not see that this nothing, this cipher, by whatever quantity it may be multiplied, remains always equal to any other cipher; they do not see that the existence of the animal individuality of every man is equally miserable and cannot be made happy by any external conditions. Men will not see that there is no one existence, no carnal existence, which can be more happy than any other; it is a law resembling that by which the waters of a lake cannot rise at any one point above the common level. Men, having their reason perverted, do not see this, but employ their perverted reason to perform this impossible task of raising the water at certain points of the surface of the lake—something like what children do when they are bathing and call it "brewing beer"—and thus they pass their whole existence.

It seems to them that the existences of men are more or less happy, desirable. The existence of a poor workman or of a sick person is sad and unhappy, they say; the life of a rich man or of a man in very good health is good and happy; and they apply all the strength of their reason to avoid a sad, unhappy, poor and sickly existence, and to create for themselves a good, rich, healthy and happy one.

Generations have laboured to find the means of arranging and keeping up these various very happy lives, and the programmes of these imagined better lives (for it is thus that men describe their animal existence) have been transmitted to us by inheritance. Men vie with each other in efforts to keep up to the best of their ability this happy *life*, the arrangements of which they have inherited successively from their ancestors, or to create for themselves a new and still happier *life*. They imagine that in maintaining this hereditary arrangement of existence, or in creating a new one yet better from their point of view, they are really doing something.

By supporting each other mutually in this illusion men often succeed in sincerely persuading themselves that life consists of this insensate beating of the water, the absurdity of which ought to be evident to every one of them; they are so convinced of it, that they repulse with scorn the entreaties of the true life, which they ceaselessly hear in the instructions of the truth, in the examples of the life of living men, and in their own stifled hearts where they can never completely stifle the voice of reason and of love.

Then occurs something extraordinary. Men, the greater number of men, having the possibility of living a life of reason and of love, are in the same position as sheep being driven out of a building on fire, and which, imagining that they will be cast into the flames, use all their strength to struggle against those who wish to save them.

Through fear of death men do not wish to escape from it; through fear of suffering, they torture themselves and deprive themselves of the only welfare and life possible to them.

CHAPTER XXVII

The fear of death is only the consciousness of the unsolved contradiction of life.

" THERE is no death," the Voice of Truth says to men. " I am the resurrection and the life; he that believeth in me, though he were dead, yet shall he live. And whosoever liveth and believeth in me shall never die. Believest thou this?"

"There is no death," all the great teachers of the world have said, and still say, and the millions of men who have comprehended the meaning of life say it also, and confirm it by their lives. It is this which every living man feels in his soul, in the lucid moments of consciousness. But the men who do not understand life cannot help being afraid of death. They see it and they believe in it.

"How, no death!" cry with indignation and anger these men;—"It is a sophism! Death is before us; it has mown down millions of men and will mow us down also. However much you say it does not exist, —it is here all the time. It is here now!" And they see this of which they speak, as the madman sees the phantom which frightens him. He cannot touch that phantom, which has never touched him, hè knows nothing of its intentions; but he has such fear and suffers so much from this vision of his imagination, that he is deprived of the possibility of living. It is the same with death. Man does not know his death and can never know it; it has never touched him, and he knows nothing of its intentions. Of what is he afraid, then?

"It has not seized me yet but it will seize me, I am quite sure,—it will seize me and annihilate me. And it is terrible," say the men who do not understand life!

If the men who have this false idea of life were capable of reasoning with calmness and sensibly, they ought, even on the basis of their own conception of life, to conclude that there is nothing disagreeable nor terrible in the idea that our carnal existence will undergo the same changes that we see accomplished incessantly in all beings, and which we call death.

I shall die. What is there terrible in that? What various changes have taken place and are now taking place in my carnal existence without my fearing them! Why should I fear this change which has not yet come on, and which not only is not repugnant to my reason and my experience but is so comprehensible, so familiar and so natural to me, that during the course of my life I have constantly created and I yet create fancies, where the death of animals and even of men is regarded by me as an indispensable and often happy condition of life? What then is there terrible?

There are but two strictly logical points of view: one false—that according to which life is understood as these visible phenomena which take place in my body from birth to death; the other true — that according to which life is understood as the invisible consciousness of it that I bear in myself. One of these points of view is erroneous, the other true, but both are logical, and men can accept the one which suits them. Both equally exclude the fear of death.

The first, false, point of view, that which understands life as the visible phenomena of the body from birth to death, is as old as the world. It is not, as many think, a view of life elaborated by the materialistic science, and the philosophy of our time; contemporary science and philosophy have only carried this common view to its utmost limits, in proving in a manner more evident than before how impossible it is to reconcile this view with the fundamental demands of human nature; but it is an old idea, primitive, common to the men who are in an inferior degree of development. It is expressed among the Chinese, the Buddhists, the Hebrews, in the book of Job, and in the sentence, " Dust thou art and unto dust shalt thou return."

In its actual form this view may be thus expressed : " Life is the fortuitous play of the forces in matter which occurs in space and time. As for what we call our consciousness, it is not life, it is only a certain illusion of the senses by which it appears that life is in that consciousness. The consciousness is a spark kindled in matter under certain conditions. This spark flares up, burns, then grows less, and ends by being extinguished altogether. This spark, which is the consciousness experienced by matter during a definite period of time between two eternities, is nothing. And although the consciousness sees itself and all the infinite world, and sits in judgment upon itself and all the infinite world, although it sees all the play of the eventualities of this world, although it calls this play—and this is the chief point—a fortuitous play, in contrast with something that is not fortuitous, this consciousness itself is nothing but a product of inanimate matter, a phantom which appears and disappears without leaving a trace or meaning. It is all the product of matter modified to its utmost; and this that we call life is but a certain condition of inanimate matter also." Such is one view of life. This view is perfectly logical. According to it, the reasonable consciousness of man is only an accident which accompanies a certain state of matter; consequently, this which in our consciousness we call life is but a phantom. That which is inanimate alone exists. This which we call life is a game of death. According to this view of life, it is not death which should be horrible, but life, because it is something unnatural, irrational; and this is what we find in the doctrines of the Buddhists and the modern pessimists, Schopenhauer and Hartmann.

The other view of life is as follows: " Life is only what I recognize in myself. But, I have always consciousness of my life, not of what I was or shall be [it is thus that I reason on my life], but I have consciousness of my life as I am—which never anywhere either begins or ends. The idea of time and space is not linked to the consciousness that I have of my life. My life is manifested in time and space,

9

but this is only a manifestation. The life of which I
have consciousness I recognize outside of time and
space.   So that this point of view is quite the
opposite of the preceding.   It is not the consciousness of life which is a phantom, but, on the contrary,
all this which is limited in time and space is illusory.
Therefore the cessation in space and in time of the
corporeal existence, according to this point of view,
is no reality, and is incapable not only of interrupting
but of troubling my true life.   Then, according to
this view, death does not exist."

Neither in the one, nor in the other of these views
of life, could the terror of death exist if men held
rigorously to the one or the other.

Man cannot fear death, either insomuch as he is
an animal, or insomuch as he is a reasonable being ;
the animal, not having the consciousness of life does
not see death ; the reasonable being, having consciousness of life, cannot see in the death of the
animal anything more than as a natural and uninterrupted movement of matter.   What man fears,
is not the death which he does not know, but life,
which his animal and reasonable being alone know.
This feeling which is expressed in men by the fear
of death is nothing but the consciousness of the
intrinsic contradiction of life, just as the terror of
the phantoms is nothing but the consciousness of a
diseased state of the mind.

" I shall cease to be.   I shall die.   All this that
constitutes my life will die," says a Voice to man.   " I
am," says another voice, " I cannot and must not die."

" I ought not to die, and yet I am dying."   It
is not in death itself, but in this contradiction that
the cause lies of the fright which seizes man at the
thought of his carnal death ; the terror of death
does not result from man's fearing the cessation of
his animal existence, but from his imagining that this
which cannot and ought not to die, dies.   To think

of future death, is only to carry into the future the idea of death which is taking place now. The vision of carnal death to come is not the awakening of the thought of death, but on the contrary the awakening of the thought of the life that man ought to have, but which he has not. This feeling is similar to what a man must experience who should come back to life in the grave, under ground. " Life exists," he would say, " and I am in death ; here is death." It seems as if that which is and ought to be is annihilated. And the human mind goes astray and is struck with fear. The best proof that fear of death is not in reality fear of death, but fear of false life, is that men often kill themselves from fear of death.

If men are frightened at the thought of carnal death, it is not that they dread that their life may end with it ; but it is that carnal death shows them clearly the necessity of the true life which they do not possess. This is why men who do not understand life do not like to think of death. For them, to think of death is to recognize that they are not living according to the demands of their reasonable consciousness. Men who fear death, fear it because they picture it as nothingness and darkness ; but they see the nothingness and darkness because they do not see the life.

CHAPTER XXVIII

Carnal death destroys the body limited in space and the consciousness limited in time, but cannot destroy that which constitutes the foundation of life : the special relationship of each being to the world.

IF the men who do not see life would only approach these phantoms which they fear, and touch them, they would see that they are phantoms — only phantoms and nothing more.

The terror of death always arises from men fearing to lose, at their carnal death, their own selves, which —they feel—form their lives.   " I shall die, my body will decompose, and I shall be annihilated. My self! that self which has lived in my body for all these years!"

Men attach much value to this self, this I, and as they suppose that this I coincides with their carnal life, they conclude that it must be destroyed at the same time as that life.   It is the most ordinary conclusion, and it is rare that anyone thinks of doubting it; yet this conclusion is quite arbitrary.

Men, those who consider themselves materialists, as well as those who consider themselves spiritualists, are so much accustomed to the idea that their real self is the consciousness of their body which has lived for a certain number of years, that it never occurs to them to verify the justice of such an assertion.

I have lived fifty-nine years, and during all that time I have had consciousness of myself in my body, and it seems to me that it is precisely this consciousness of myself that has been my life.   And yet this is but an illusion.   I have lived : neither fifty-nine years, nor fifty-nine thousand years, nor fifty-nine seconds. Neither my body nor the term of its existence can in any manner determine the life of my self.   If I, at any instant of my life, ask myself consciously " What am I?" I shall reply, " Something which thinks and feels," that is, something related to the world in a manner quite special to myself.   It is this only that I recognize as myself, and nothing else.   As for knowing when and where I was born, when and where I began to feel and think as I do now think and feel, of this I know nothing positive at all.   My consciousness says to me simply—I exist, and I am in relationship with the world where I find myself now.   As about my birth, infancy, the

numerous phases of youth and middle-age, and even
of a later period, I often do not remember anything.
And even if I have some reminiscence of my past,
or if I am reminded of it, I recall it or I remember
it much as if it were told me about other people.
Therefore what right have I to declare that during
the whole of my existence I have been *one single I*?
My body is not single and never has been : my body
always has been and still is matter ceaselessly flowing
through something immaterial and invisible which
recognizes this which flows through it as my body.
My entire body has been changed every ten years ;
nothing of the old has remained : the muscles, the
intestines, the bones, and the brain—all have been
transformed.

My body is one only, because there exists something immaterial which recognizes as its exclusive
property all this changing body. This immateriality
is that which we call consciousness : it alone
maintains the unity of the body and recognizes it
as its property. If I had not the consciousness that
I am a being distinct from all the rest, I should
never know anything of my life or of any other life.
That is why it appears to me at first sight that the
basis of all, that is to say consciousness, ought to be
constant. But, neither is this true ; consciousness is
not constant. During our whole life, and even now,
we see recur the phenomenon of sleep which seems
to us very simple, because we all sleep every day,
but which is absolutely incomprehensible if we grant
(what it is impossible not to grant) that during sleep
consciousness sometimes ceases entirely.

Every day, during deep sleep, consciousness ceases
entirely, then it is renewed again. And yet this
consciousness is the one principle which maintains
the unity of the whole body and recognizes it as its
own. It seems as if when consciousness ceases the
body ought also to dissolve and to lose its distinct

state; but that does not happen either in natural or artificial sleep.

Moreover, not only does the consciousness which maintains the unity of the body disappear periodically without the body becoming dissolved, but consciousness also changes like the body. Just as there is nothing in common between the substance of my body, as it was ten years ago, and as it is now, as there has not been one body, so there has not been in me one consciousness. My consciousness, when I was a child three years old, and that of the present, are as different as is the matter of my present body and that of thirty years ago. There is not a single consciousness, but there is a series of successive consciousnesses which one can divide to infinity.

Consequently this consciousness which maintains the unity of the body and recognizes it as its own, is not something single, but something interrupted and changing. Just as a man has not a single body, so he has not within himself a single consciousness as we ordinarily imagine. There is not one and the same body in man, nor one and the same feature which distinguishes this body from every other; there is not one single consciousness during the whole life of one man, but there is a series of successive consciousnesses bound together by something; and yet man feels himself to be himself.

Our body is not single, and that which recognizes this changing body as one and ours is not continuous in duration; it is but a series of consciousnesses which change, and often already we have lost both our body and these consciousnesses; we constantly lose the body, we also lose our consciousness every day when we go to sleep; every day and every hour we feel in us the changes of this consciousness without experiencing the least fear.

Thus then, if there is any such thing as our *I*,

which we fear to lose at death, this *I* does not lie either in this body which we call ours, nor in this consciousness which we call ours during a certain time, but it must be in that which unites in one the whole series of successive consciousnesses. But what then is this something which unites all the consciousnesses which succeed each other in duration of time? What is this radical and particular *I* which does not consist of the existence of my body or of the series of consciousnesses which have appeared in it, this chief *I* on which come threading themselves, one after another, as on a knitting-needle, the different consciousnesses, which succeed each other in duration? The question appears very profound and very wise, and yet there is not a child who could not reply to it, and who would not do so twenty times a day. " I like this, but I do not like that."

These words are very simple, and yet they solve the question of how to know which is the particular self which links all the consciousnesses. It is this self which likes this but does not like that. Why we like this and do not like that, no one knows, and it is exactly this which forms the basis of the life of every man, and which unites in one all the diverse successive states of consciousness of each individual man. The exterior world acts in the same manner on all men. But the impressions of men, even when placed in absolutely identical conditions, vary infinitely, as much in the number received and the capability of being divided into infinite sub-impressions as in their intensity. It is these impressions which form the series of successive consciousnesses of every man. But all these successive consciousnesses are united only because in the present some impressions act, whilst others do not act on the consciousness of any one man. The reason why certain impressions act or do not act on any one man is found only in the disposition of the man to love more or less this or that.

-It is only as a result of the greater or less degree of liking for certain things, that one certain series of consciousnesses is formed in the man and not another. It is only in the faculty of loving one thing more or less and not loving another that the particular and essential self of man consists, the self in which are grouped in one all the scattered and interrupted consciousnesses. And this faculty of liking this more and that less, although it is developed during our life, has been transmitted to us in this life already fully formed by an invisible and unknown past.

This particular quality of man to love in a more or less degree one thing, and not to love another, is usually called the character. Under this word is often understood the peculiarity of the qualities of each individual man which result from certain conditions of place and time. But this is wrong. The essential quality of man, to love more or less one thing and not to love another, does not depend on conditions of time and space; quite the contrary, if the conditions of time and space act or do not act on man it is only because he has already, when he comes into the world, a very decided inclination to like this and not to like that. This is why men born and educated in conditions of time and space entirely identical, often present the greatest contrast in their interior self.

The bond which unites all the scattered consciousnesses, which latter in their turn unite our body, is something very definite, although independent of the conditions of time and space; we bring it with us into the world from a region outside of time and space; and this *something*, which consists in a certain exclusive relationship of my being to the world, is my only veritable and true self. I only know myself as a certain exclusive relationship to the world, and if I know other men, it is only in considering them as particular relationships to the world. No one entering into close spiritual communication with men, allows himself to be guided by external signs, but endeavours to penetrate into their essence, that is, to know what is their relationship to the world, what they love and what they do not love and in what degree.

If I know each separate animal : horse, dog, cow ; if ever I enter into serious spiritual communication with them, it is not by their external appearance but by my knowing the particular relationship to the world in which each of them stands, what each one likes or does not like and to what degree. If I know the different kinds of animals, it is really not so much by their external appearance as because each one (lion, fish, spider) presents a special relationship to the world common to all the beings of the same kind. All lions in general like one thing, all fishes another, all spiders a third ; it is only because they like different things that they are separated in my mind into living beings distinct from one another.

But this fact that I do not distinguish the special relationship with the world of each one of these beings of the same kind, does not prove that the particular relationship does not exist, but only that the life of a particular spider is so far removed from the relationship to the world in which I find myself, that I have not been able to comprehend it, as Silvio Pellico comprehended his particular spider.

The basis of all the knowledge that I have of myself and of the whole world, is this special relationship to the world in which I find myself, that enables me to see other beings who find themselves also in a special relationship to the world.

But my relationship to the world was not set up in this life, nor did it begin with my body nor with the series of consciousnesses which succeed each other in time, but was prior to them.

Consequently, my body, which is united in a whole by my temporary consciousness, can be destroyed, my temporary consciousness itself can be destroyed; but what cannot be destroyed is my particular relationship to the world; that is to say, that which forms my distinct self which has created for me all that exists. It cannot be destroyed because it alone exists. If it did not exist, I should not know either the series of my successive consciousnesses, nor my body, nor my life, nor any other life. Consequently the destruction of the body and of the consciousness cannot be any evidence of the annihilation of my special relationship to the world, a relationship which did not begin and has not arisen in this life.

CHAPTER XXIX

Men fear death because they have restricted life by their false conception, taking a part of life to be the whole.

WE fear to lose at our carnal death our special *I* which unites in a whole the body and the series of consciousnesses which manifest themselves in time; and yet my special *I* did not begin at my birth; therefore the cessation of a certain temporary consciousness could not destroy this which unites all the temporary consciousnesses.

Carnal death destroys effectually this which maintains the unity of the body, the consciousness of the temporary life. But has not this happened incessantly and every day when we have gone to sleep? The whole question is that of knowing whether carnal death destroys' this which unites in one all the successive consciousnesses, that is to say my particular relationship to the world? Before deciding in the affirmative, we should have first to prove that this special relationship to the world, which unites all the successive consciousnesses, is born with my carnal existence, and therefore dies with it. And this it is impossible to do.

If I take my consciousness for the basis of my reasoning, I see that this which unites all my consciousnesses, that is to say a certain sympathy towards one thing, and a coldness towards another, this which makes one thing remain in me and another disappear, the degree of my love for good, of my hatred for evil,—I see, I say, that this particular relationship to the world which exactly constitutes myself, my special Self, is not the product of some external cause, but is the fundamental cause of all the other phenomena of my life.

If I take observation for the basis of my reasoning, it certainly seems to me at first that the causes of the distinctive character of my special Self are in the distinctive character of my parents and in the conditions which have influenced them. But continuing to reason in this way, I cannot avoid seeing that if my special Self lies in the distinctive character of my parents and in the conditions which have influenced them, it lies also in the character of all my ancestors and in the conditions of their existence, and so on indefinitely, that is to say beyond time and space; so that my special Self has arisen outside of time and space, and it is precisely this Self of which I have consciousness.

It is only this basis, outside of time and space, this basis of my special relationship to the world, which unites all the consciousnesses I can remember and those which have preceded the life I remember [as Plato says, and as we all feel in ourselves], it is on this basis, I say, of my special relationship to the world, that the special *I*, of which we fear the destruction at our carnal death, exists.

But it is enough to understand that this which unites all the consciousnesses, this which forms the special *I* of every man, is outside of time, always has existed and does exist; it is enough to understand that this which can be interrupted, is only the series of consciousnesses of a certain time, in order to see clearly that the destruction of the last consciousness in chronological order, at the time of carnal death, is as powerless to destroy the true human Self as is the daily sleep. There is not a single man who fears to go to sleep, although in sleep the same phenomenon takes place as in death: the cessation of consciousness in time. Man does not fear to go to sleep, although in sleep the consciousness is as completely interrupted as in death; and if he does not feel fear, it is not because he has a conviction that he will awake again, as he has slept and awakened before; this reasoning is false, because he might go to sleep a thousand times and not wake up the thousand and first time. Man never reasons thus, and this argument could not reassure him; but man knows that his true Self lives outside of time, and therefore that the cessation of his consciousness which is manifested for him in time cannot disturb his life.

If man could go to sleep for a thousand years, as in the fairy tales, he would go to sleep as tranquilly as for two hours. To the consciousness of non-temporal life, of the true life, there is no difference between a pause of a thousand years in time, and a pause of eight hours, because time for such a life does not exist.

The destruction of the body results in the destruction of the present consciousness.

It is time men accustomed themselves to the modifications of the body and to the successive changes of temporary consciousnesses. These changes commenced when man first had consciousness of himself, and have taken place without interruption since. Man does not fear the changes which take place in his body, and not only is he not afraid of them, but very often he desires their acceleration; he desires to grow, to attain manhood, he desires the healing of his wounds. Man was once nothing but a mass of red flesh, and his consciousness consisted in the demands of his stomach; now he is a man bearded and reasonable, or a woman loving her grown-up children. The body and the consciousness are entirely changed, and the man has not been frightened by those changes which have brought him to his present condition, on the contrary he has often desired them. What is there, then, terrible in the change which must take place when death comes?

Destruction? But this which presides over these changes, this special relationship to the world, this in which the consciousness of the true life consists, did not commence at the birth of the body, but outside of the body and outside of time. Consequently how could a change in time and space destroy that which is outside of time and space?

Man fixes his attention on a very small piece of his life, he will not look at his life as a complete whole, and he trembles at the idea of losing from sight this very small piece which he cherishes. It reminds me of the story of the madman who believed himself to be made of glass. One day when he fell down he cried " Crash !" and died at once. To possess life, man must take the whole of it, and not that small part of it which is manifested in time and space. He who will take the whole of life shall receive more; but he who takes a part of it only shall be deprived of that which he has.

CHAPTER XXX

Life is a relationship to the world. The movement of life is the establishment of new and loftier relationships, hence death is the introduction to a new relationship.

WE cannot conceive of life otherwise than as a certain relationship to the world ; it is thus that we conceive of it in ourselves and also in other beings.

But, in ourselves, we understand life not only as a once-existing relationship to the world, but also as the establishment of a new relationship, by means of the increasing submission of the animal individuality to reason, and the manifestation of a greater degree of love. The inevitable destruction of the carnal existence which we observe in ourselves, shows us that our relationship to the world in which we find ourselves is not constant, but that we are obliged to establish others. The establishment of these new relationships, that is to say the movement of life, destroys the idea of death.

Death can only present itself to that man who, not recognizing his life as the establishment of a rational relationship to the world, manifested in himself by a greater and greater love, has made no change in that relationship, that is to say remains in the same degree of love for one thing and aversion for another with which he entered into existence.

Life is an incessant movement. The man who makes no change in his relationship to the world, that is to say remains in the same degree of love as at his entrance into life, feels the cessation of life, and death presents itself to him. It is only to such a man that death is visible and terrible. His whole existence is nothing but a continual death. Death is visible and terrible to him, not only in the future but also in the present, every time the decay of the animal life is manifested to him, from infancy to old age. Whilst the march of existence from infancy to maturity appears to be a temporary increase of the physical forces, in reality the limbs are but hardening, the suppleness and vitality of the body go on diminishing, and this without interruption from birth to death. Such a man has death constantly before his eyes, and nothing can save him from it. From day to day and from hour to hour the position of such a man grows worse and worse, and nothing can ameliorate it. He regards only his special relationship to the world, that is to say his love for one thing and aversion for another, as one of the conditions of his existence; whilst the important affair of life, the establishment of a new relationship to the world, the growth of love, seems to him something unnecessary. All his life is passed in vain efforts to avoid the inevitable failure of life, its hardening and infirmity, decrepitude, and death.

Not so with the man who understands life. This man knows that he has brought into his present life, from a past which is unknown to him, his special relationship to the world, that is to say his liking for one thing, his dislike for another. He knows that this love for one thing, this aversion for another, that he brought with him into his existence, is the very essence of his life; he knows that it is not an accidental peculiarity of his life, but that in this alone is the movement of life, and it is only in this movement, that is to say in the increase of love, that he places his life.

Considering his past in this life, he sees, in remembering successive consciousnesses, that his relationship to the world has been modified, that submission to the law of reason has grown, that the strength and the extension of love have gone on increasing, giving him more and more welfare independently, and sometimes even in spite of the

proportional decay of the individual existence. This
man, who has received his life from an unseen past,
and who is conscious of a constant and uninterrupted
growth, carries it on not only with calmness, but
with joy, into an invisible future.

People say : disease, old age, decrepitude, falling
into second childhood, destroy the consciousness and
the life of man.   Of which man ?   I picture to myself
St. John the Evangelist according to tradition, fallen
from old age into second childhood.   He, according
to tradition, uttered only these words, " Brothers, love
one another."   This old man, hardly able to move,
his eyes full of tears, mumbled only these three
words, " Love one another."   With such a man the
animal existence gives no more than a feeble
glimmer, it has been entirely absorbed by a new
relationship to the world, by a new living being
which has not yet found a place in the existence of
the carnal man.

For the man who understands his life where it
really is, to distress himself because he sees this life
diminishing in consequence of disease and old age,
is as if a man were to be distressed on seeing his
shadow diminish as he approaches the light.   To
believe in the destruction of one's life, because the
body is destroyed, is to believe that the disappearance of the shadow of an object, when it enters into
full light, is a sure proof of the destruction of the
object itself.   Such a conclusion can only be accepted
by that man who has for so long a time looked at the
shadow that he has ended by taking it for the
object itself.

To the man who knows himself, not only by the
reflection of the limited existence in time and space,
but by the growth of his relationship of love to
the world—to this man, I say, the disappearance of
the shadow, of the conditions of time and space, is
only the indication of a greater degree of light.   It

is as impossible to the man who regards his life as a
certain special relationship to the world, which he
brought with him when entering into existence, and
which has been developed during his life by the
growth of love—it is as impossible to this man, I
say, to believe in his own destruction, as it is impossible to one who knows the external and visible
laws of the world, to believe that his mother found
him under a cabbage leaf, or that his body will
suddenly fly away no one knows where, and nothing
remain of it.

CHAPTER XXXI

The life of men when they are dead does not cease in this world.

But still more clearly, I will not say, from another
point of view, but—according to the very essence of
life as we know it, does death become a superstition.
My friend, my brother, lived the same life as myself
and now he has ceased to live this life. His life was
his consciousness, and it was subjected to the conditions of his corporeal existence ; consequently, his
consciousness can no longer manifest itself in space
and in time—it no longer exists for me. My brother
has existed, I have been in communication with him,
now he is no more, and I cannot tell where he is.
" Every link between him and us is broken. He no
longer exists for us, just as we shall no longer exist
for those who will remain. What is this then, if not
death ? "

So men speak who do not understand life ; they
see in the cessation of external communication the
most irrefutable proof of the reality of death. And
yet in nothing is the illusion of the idea of death
dissipated more clearly and more evidently than

10

in the cessation of the carnal existence of their
neighbours.

My brother is dead. What then has happened?
This is what has happened : the manifestation of his
relationship to the world, which I could observe in
space and time, has disappeared from my sight and
nothing is left.

" Nothing is left,"—this is what the chrysalis, the
cocoon, would say before the release of the butterfly,
on seeing the neighbouring cocoon left empty. And
the cocoon would be right in speaking thus if it
were capable of thinking and speaking, because,
having lost its neighbour, it would indeed be unable
in any way to feel it. But this is not so with man.
My brother is dead; his cocoon, in truth, is left
empty; I no longer see him in that form which I
have seen him until to-day, but his disappearance
from my sight has not destroyed my relationship to
him. His memory has been left—as we are accustomed to say.

The memory which is preserved, is not the memory
of his hands, face, eyes, but that of his spiritual image.

What is this memory? This so simple and so
intelligible a word? The forms of crystals and of
animals disappear and there remains among them
no memory. But I, I remember my friend and
brother. And this memory is just so much the
more vivid as the life of my friend and brother has
been more conformed to the law of reason, and the
more it has been manifested in love. This memory
is not only an idea, but it acts on me exactly in the
same manner as the life of my brother did during his
earthly existence. This memory is the same invisible
and immaterial atmosphere that surrounded his life
and acted on me and on others during his carnal
existence, in the same manner as it acts on me still
after his death. This memory demands of me after
his death now the same as it demanded of me before

his death. Indeed, this memory becomes more obligatory for me after his death than it was during his life. The vital force which was in my brother, far from disappearing and diminishing, has only undergone a transformation ; it has increased, and acts on me with more force than before.

The force of his life acts after his carnal death, with as much intensity and even more than before his death, and it acts as everything does which is really alive. Consequently, since I experience the influence of this vital force now as really as I experienced it during the carnal existence of my brother (that is as his relationship which united him to the world and explained to me my own relationship to the world), what right have I to affirm that my dead brother no longer possesses life ? All that I can say is, that he is gone out of the inferior relationship to the world in which he was as an animal, and in which I still find myself. I do not see the centre of the new relationship to the world in which he finds himself now, but I cannot deny his life, because I feel his action upon me. The mirror showed me the links which bound me to this man ; the mirror is darkened. I no longer perceive the links which bind me to him, but I feel, with all my being, that he holds me just as before, and therefore that he exists.

Indeed, this life, invisible to me, of my dead brother, not only acts upon me, but penetrates me. His special living Self, his relationship to the world, is identified with my own. In the establishment of my relationship to the world he raises me to the step which he has himself reached, and my special living Self distinguishes more clearly the higher steps to which he has now mounted ; he is hidden from my eyes, but he draws me to himself. Thus I know for myself the life of my brother who has died the carnal death, and this is why I cannot doubt that

his life has not ceased.   In observing, on the other
hand, the action on the world of this life which has
disappeared from my eyes, I acquire a yet deeper
conviction of its reality.   The man is dead, but his
relationship to the world continues to act upon men ;
its action is not only what it was during life, but, in
many cases, it is yet more intense ; it increases and
grows as everything that is alive does, in proportion
to its advanced state of reason and of love, without
ever ceasing and without any interruption.

It is long since Christ died ; his carnal existence
was short and we have no clear idea of his carnal
individuality ; but the strength of his life of reason
and of love, his relationship to the world (and no
other cause), exercises to-day an influence on millions
of men who accept this relationship to the world
and conform their life to it.   What is it which acts
thus ?   What is this thing which, joined formerly to
the carnal existence of Christ, produces the continua-
tion and the expansion of this same life?   We say
that it is not the life of Christ but its consequences.
And in saying these words, which have no meaning,
it appears to us that we have said something much
more clear and precise than if we had said that this
force is the living Christ himself.   This is just what
the ants might say which had dug around an acorn
that has grown and has become an oak ; the acorn
has grown and has become an oak, it pierces the
ground with its roots, it throws out branches, leaves,
new acorns, it intercepts the light, and the rain, and
changes everything that lives around it.   " It is not
the life of the acorn," the ants might say, " but the
consequences of it ; its life came to an end when we
carried it away and buried it in a hole."

My brother died yesterday or a thousand years
ago, and this same vital force which acted during
his carnal existence, continues to act yet more
strongly on me and on hundreds of thousands and

millions of men, although the centre of this force of
his temporary carnal existence visible to me has
disappeared from my eyes. What does this matter?
I have seen the light of the dry grass which burned
before me; the grass is burnt out, but the light has
only increased; I do not see the cause of that light,
I do not know what burns, but I can conclude that
the fire which consumed the grass now consumes a
forest afar or something which I cannot see. But
such is the light, that not only do I see it now, but
it guides me and gives me life. And I live by this
light. How then can I deny its existence? I may
believe that the force of this life has now another
centre, invisible to me. But I may not deny its
existence, because I feel it and it makes me live.
What this centre is, what this life in itself is, I cannot know; I may try to guess, if I like guessing and
if I am not afraid of going astray. But when I wish
to have a rational conception of life, I content myself
with what is clear and indubitable, and do not seek
to spoil what is clear and indubitable by adding
obscure and arbitrary conjectures. It is enough for
me to know that all that by which I live is composed
of the life of all the men who have lived before me
and who are long since dead,—and therefore that
the man who accomplished the law of his life in
subjecting his animal individuality to reason and in
manifesting the strength of his love, has lived and
lives in other men after the disappearance of his
carnal existence,—it is enough for me to know this,
I say, for the absurd and terrible superstition about
death to cease for ever from tormenting me.

In studying the men who leave behind them a
force which continues to act, we can see why these
men, in subjecting their individuality to reason and
in giving themselves up to a life of love, never could
doubt and never have doubted the impossibility of
the destruction of life.

We can also find in the life of such people the
foundation of their belief in the non-interruption of
life, and afterwards in closely studying our own lives
we can find this foundation in ourselves also.   Christ
said that he will live after the disappearance of the
phantom of life.   He said this because, during his
carnal existence, he had already entered into this
true life which cannot cease.   During his carnal
existence he already lived in the midst of rays of
light from that other centre of life towards which he
was advancing, and he saw, during his life, that the
rays of this light already lit up the men around him.
This is what every man sees who has renounced
individuality and who lives a life of reason and of
love.

However narrow may be the sphere of activity of
the man,—be he a Christ, a Socrates, a good man,
an unknown man, an old man, a young man, a
woman,—if he lives in renouncing his individuality
for the welfare of others, he already enters here,
during this life, into that new relationship to the
world for which there is no death, and the establishment of which is the one important business of this
life for all men.

Man whose life rests in submission to the law of
reason, and in the manifestation of love, sees, even
in this life, on the one side the rays of light from
this new centre of life towards which he goes; and,
on the other, the action which this light, in passing
through him, produces on those by whom he is
surrounded ; and this gives him an indubitable faith
in the stability, immortality, and eternal growth of
life.   Faith in immortality cannot be received by
everyone ; one cannot convince oneself of immortality.   Before this faith can exist there must be
immortality, and for immortality to exist one must
understand what makes our life immortal.   Faith in
future life is possible only when one has accomplished

one's task of life, and established in this life that new relationship to the world which does not yet find a place in it.

CHAPTER XXXII

The dread of death proceeds from man's confusion of his different relationships to the world.

Yes, if we consider life in its true meaning, it becomes difficult even to understand on what the strange dread of death rests.

Just as, when you examine what frightened you in the darkness, as a phantom, you cannot again by any means restore that visionary fear.

The fear of losing what alone exists, is caused entirely by life presenting itself to man, not merely in the particular relationship known, though invisible, of the reasonable consciousness to the world, but in two relationships unknown but visible to him : that of his animal consciousness and that of his body. All that exists presents itself to man under three different aspects, which are : 1st, The relationship of his reasonable consciousness to the world ; 2nd, the relationship of his animal consciousness to the world ; and, 3rd, the relationship of the substance of his body to the world. Not understanding that the relationship of his reasonable consciousness to the world is his only life, man imagines that his life consists also in the visible relationship of his animal consciousness, and of matter, to the world, and he fears to lose this particular relationship of the reasonable consciousness when the former relationship to the world of his animal self and of the matter which composes it come to be disturbed in his individuality.

It seems to him that he himself is the product

of the evolution of matter which has reached the degree of the individual animal consciousness. It seems to him that this animal consciousness is transformed into a reasonable consciousness, that this becomes enfeebled in turn, and becomes animal again ; finally that the animal consciousness becoming enfeebled returns to the inanimate matter whence it had been drawn. Through looking at things in this way the relationship of his reasonable consciousness to the world seems to him something fortuitous, useless; and perishable. The consequence of this false conception is that the relationship of the animal consciousness of man to the world appears to be indestructible—the animal perpetuates itself in its species ; and also that the relationship of matter to the world cannot in any manner be destroyed, but seems to be eternal. The most precious thing of all—the reasonable consciousness of man—not only is not eternal, but is merely the reflection of something useless and superfluous.

And man feels that this cannot be true. Hence comes the fear of death. To escape the horror which this causes, some force themselves to believe that the animal consciousness actually is their reasonable consciousness, and that the idea of the immortality of the man-animal, that is to say of his species and his descendants, is enough to satisfy the demand of the immortality of the reasonable consciousness which they bear in themselves. Others seek to persuade themselves that the life, which had never existed before, after its sudden appearance in the carnal form and its disappearance from that form, shall be raised from the dead in the flesh and shall live. But for men who do not recognize life in the relationship of the reasonable consciousness to the world, it is impossible to believe either the one or the other of these two opinions. It is clear that for them the perpetuation of the human race cannot satisfy the incessant demand for an eternal special Self: but the idea of life beginning over again implies that of the cessation of life, and if life has not existed in the past, has not existed always, then it cannot exist after.

For the one class as for the other, earthly life is a wave. Individuality emerges from inanimate matter, from the individuality comes the reasonable consciousness, that is, the summit of the wave. Having reached its culminating point, the wave, that is the reasonable consciousness and the individuality, return to their starting-point and annihilate themselves. For the one class, as for the other, human life is the visible life. Man has grown, has arrived at maturity, has died; after his death nothing can exist henceforth for him; all that remains after him, his descendants, even his own actions, cannot satisfy him. He pities *himself*. He fears the cessation of *his* life. He cannot believe that his life, which has begun here on the earth in his body and has ceased here, that this life which is his own shall be raised again.

Man knows that if he has not existed before, and if he came out of nothingness and died, his special Self will cease to exist, nor can it exist. . Man will only know that he is immortal when he understands that he was never born, that he has always been, is, and will be. Man will not believe in his immortality until he understands that his life is not a wave, but an eternal movement which is only manifested in this life under the form of a wave.

I foresee that I shall die, and that my life will cease, and this thought tortures me and frightens me, because I pity myself. But what will die? What do I pity? What am I myself from the most ordinary point of view? First of all I am flesh. What then? I am afraid of losing this, this is what I regret? It is proved not to be so; that not a bit of the body, of matter, can be lost. Then, this part of myself is protected, I have no cause to fear that it will be lost. Nothing will be lost. But, it seems, this is not what one deplores. It is myself who am to be pitied, I, Leo, Ivan. But no one is now what he was twenty years ago, and every day he is different. In what manner then, do I pity myself? No, they say, it is not that. I do not pity this. I pity my consciousness, my self, my *Ego*.

But your consciousness has not always been one; there have been several; a year ago, it was not the same that it is to-day; ten years ago, it differed still more; at a still farther period it was entirely different; as far as you can remember it has always gone on changing. Why do you principally regret the consciousness of to-day, and why do you so much fear to lose it? If you had never had but one, your regrets would have had some reason for existence, but this consciousness has done nothing but change incessantly. You cannot see its starting-point, and you cannot discover it anywhere, and yet you suddenly want it never to come to an end; you would like this consciousness which is now in you to exist eternally. From the moment when you first knew yourself, you have not ceased to advance. You entered into this life without knowing how; you only know that you came with this special Self which you are, that then you walked on, walked on, and have reached half-way. And suddenly, neither glad nor afraid, you resist and do not wish to budge from the place; you will not advance because you do not perceive what is beyond. You have not seen the place whence you came, and this into which you have entered, and yet you have come; you came in by the entrance gate, and you do not wish to go out by the departure gate.

All your life has been a march through carnal existence; you have walked, you have hurried on, and behold all at once you experience regrets in seeing the accomplishment of what you have been doing all the time. You are frightened at the idea of the great change which must come on with carnal death : but a change quite as great took place at your birth, and not only has nothing unpleasant resulted, but, on the contrary, such happiness has resulted that you never wish to be separated from it.

What can frighten you? You say that you regret your self with its present feelings, its thoughts, its conception of the world, its actual relationship to the world. You fear to lose your relationship to the world. What is this relationship? In what does it consist?

If it consists in your eating, drinking, and begetting, in building houses, and dressing yourself, in having entered into such and such relations with other people and with the animals, this is just the relationship which every man, in so much as he is an animal endowed with intelligence, has with life ; and this relationship cannot disappear ; millions of such relationships have existed, do exist, and will exist, and the species preserves itself as certainly and indubitably as does every atom of matter. The preservation of the species is as strongly rooted in all animals ; therefore it is so stable that there is no fear for it. If you are an animal you have nothing to fear ; if you are matter, you are still more assured of being eternal.

If you fear to lose that which is not animal, then you fear to lose your special rational relationship to the world,—that with which you entered into this existence. But you know perfectly well that that relationship did not commence with your birth, but that its relationship existed independently of the birth of your animal self, and consequently cannot depend on its death

CHAPTER XXXIII

The visible life is a part of the infinite movement of life.

My earthly life and that of all other men presents itself to me thus: All living men, including myself, find themselves here in a certain definite relationship to the world, and have reached a certain degree of love. It seems to us at first that our relationship to the world marks the commencement of our life; but, in observing ourselves and others, we see that this relationship to the world, the degree of love of each one of us, did not begin with this life, but has been brought by us into life from a past which our carnal birth hides from us; besides, we see that the whole course of our life here is but an incessant increase, a growth of our love, which is not interrupted but which is only hidden from our sight by carnal death.

Our visible life appears to me like a segment of a cone, of which the apex and the base are hidden from my mental sight. The narrowest part of the cone is my relationship to the world when for the first time I have consciousness of myself; the widest part is the highest relationship to life to which I have now attained. The beginning of this cone— its apex—is hidden from me in time by my birth; the prolongation of the cone is hidden from me by a future equally invisible in my carnal existence and in my carnal death. I see neither the apex nor the base of this cone; but when I examine the part which is traversed by my visible life, the part I remember, I recognize its nature in a positive manner. It seems to me at first that this segment of the cone is all my life; but, in proportion as the true life progresses, I see, on the one hand, that what forms the basis of my life is to be found behind it, beyond its limits; in proportion to my degree of life I have a more vivid and clear consciousness of the link which unites me to a past that I do not see. On the other hand, I see that this same basis rests on a future which is hidden from me, and I feel more clearly and vividly the link which binds me to the future; therefore I conclude that the visible life, my earthly life, is but a little part of my whole life which undoubtedly exists beyond its two extremities, before birth and after death, but which is concealed from my present understanding. Consequently the cessation of the visibility of life after carnal death, no more than its invisibility before birth can take away from me the firm conviction that it has existed before birth and that it will exist after death. I bring with me, in entering into life, a certain natural faculty of love to the world outside me; my carnal existence, whatever be its duration, passes in augmenting this love brought by me into life; and therefore I conclude with certainty that I lived before my birth and that I shall live as surely after this present moment in which I, reasoning, find myself now, as after every other moment before my carnal death.

When I look outside myself at the carnal beginnings and endings of the existences of other men [and even of beings in general], I see that one life is, so to speak, longer, another shorter; one appeared sooner and I see it for a longer time; another appeared later and disappeared very quickly again from my eyes; but, in both alike, I see the manifestation of the one law common to all true life, that is, the augmentation of love and the dispersion of the rays of life. The curtain which hides from me the temporary course of the life of men falls a little sooner or a little later, but the life of all men is the same, and, like all life, it has neither beginning nor end. And the fact that a man has lived a longer or shorter time in the conditions of existence visible to me cannot have an influence in any way on his true life. Because one man passes more slowly, another more quickly, across the field of my vision, this does not give me the right to attribute more real life to the first and less to the second. When I see a man pass before my window I know incontestably, whatever his pace may be, that this man existed before the moment when I saw him, and that he will continue to exist after I shall have lost sight of him.

But why do some pass quickly and others slowly? Why does a withered old man, morally hardened, incapable, as it seems to us, of accomplishing the law of life, which is the growth of love, why does this old man live on, whilst the child, the young man, the girl, the man, in all the strength of their intellectual activity, die, going out of the conditions of this carnal life, at the moment when, as it seems to us, they were beginning to establish in themselves a rational relationship to life?

One can understand the death of Pascal, of Gogol; but Chénier, Lermontoff, and the thousands of others whose intrinsic work had hardly begun and who would have been able, as it seems, to have accomplished so much here—What of them?

But it is only an illusion. None of us know the principles of life which others have brought into the world, nor the movement of life which fulfils itself in their life. We know still less of the obstacles to the movement of life which are met with in this or that being, and, chiefly, those other conditions of life possible, but invisible to our eyes, which cause the life of such or such a man to be ready for another existence.

When we watch a blacksmith at work it seems to us that the horseshoe is quite ready and that he has but to strike it again once or twice, but the blacksmith breaks it and throws it into the fire, because he knows that it is not yet ready.

We cannot tell whether or no the work of the true life is being accomplished in a man. We only know it in as far as it concerns us. It seems to us that the man died prematurely, but in reality it is not so. Man only dies when it is indispensable for his welfare; just as he grows, arrives at manhood only when it is necessary for his welfare.

And, in fact, if we give the name of life to the reality and not to the shadow, if the true life is the foundation of all, this foundation cannot depend on what it produces; the cause cannot proceed from the effect; the course of true life cannot be disturbed by the changes which come about in its manifestation. The movement of the life of man in this world, a movement begun but not ended, cannot be stopped because of an abscess, a microbe, or a pistol-shot.

Man dies only because the welfare of his true life cannot increase further in this world; not because he has consumption or cancer, because someone has fired a pistol at him or thrown a bomb. We habitually imagine that it is natural to live the carnal life, but that it is not natural to perish by fire, water, cold, lightning, disease, a pistol-shot, or a bomb; but one has only to reflect seriously, in considering objectively the lives of men, to see, on the contrary, that it is altogether extraordinary that man can live the carnal life in the midst of these disastrous conditions, in the midst of these innumerable microbes spread everywhere, most of them deadly. It is natural that he should perish. Therefore, in the midst of these disastrous conditions, carnal life is on the contrary something quite extraordinary from the material point of view. If we live it is not at all because we take care of ourselves, but because the work of life which regulates all these conditions is being accomplished in us. We live, not because we take care of our body, but because we are accomplishing the work of life. When this work is achieved, nothing can any longer stop the incessant decay of the human-animal life ; this decay becomes complete, and one of the proximate causes of carnal death, which always surround the man, appears to us to be the exclusive cause of his death.

Our true life exists, it is the only life we know, it is by it alone that we know the animal life ; consequently if the phantom of the true life is subjected to immutable laws, how should not the true life, which is the cause of this phantom, be subjected to laws ? But what troubles us is that we do not see the causes and the action of our true life as we see the causes and the action of exterior phenomena ; we do not know why such a man, in entering into life, brings a Self endowed with diverse faculties, why such another brings a Self endowed with different faculties, why the life of the one breaks down whilst that of the other continues. We ask ourselves what were the pre-natal causes which led to my being born such as I am ? And what will happen after death if I live this way or some other way ? And we are distressed because we do not receive an answer to these questions.

To distress myself because I cannot know now what preceded my life and what will follow my death, is as if I were to be distressed because I cannot discern what is beyond the reach of my sight. In fact, if I should perceive what is beyond the reach of my eyes, I should not see what is within the field of their vision. What is necessary before everything, for the welfare of my animal body, is to see what is around me.

It is the same with reason by means of which I understand. If I could perceive what is beyond the limits of my reason, I should not perceive what is within its sphere. But for the welfare of my true life it is necessary before all that I should know to what I ought *here* and *now* to submit my animal individuality in order to obtain the welfare of life. This is what reason shows me; it shows to me in this life the only path towards the welfare which never ends.

It shows in a positive manner that this life did not begin at birth, but has been and is always; it shows that the welfare of life grows, augments here, and reaches those boundaries which cannot contain it, and that then only it goes beyond those conditions which hinder its augmentation, passing into another existence.

Reason places man in that one path of life which, like a tunnel of conical form which goes on widening between the walls that enclose it on all sides, opens to him in the distance the indubitable eternity of life and its welfare.

CHAPTER XXXIV

The incomprehensibility of the sufferings of earthly existence proves to man more convincingly than anything that his life is not that of the individuality which begins at birth and ends at death.

BUT if man were able not to fear death and not to think about it, these horrible objectless sufferings, which nothing can justify and which cannot be averted, these sufferings which he endures, will be sufficient to cancel alone all the reasonable meaning attributed to life.

I am occupied in a good work, incontestably useful to others, and suddenly a disease seizes me, interrupts my work, exhausts me and torments me without any reason. A bolt has grown rusty in the rails and it slips out the day a train passes; in one carriage is a good woman—a mother, and her children are crushed before her eyes. An earthquake destroys just that place where Lisbon or Vierny stands, and innocent men are buried alive in the earth and die in horrible sufferings. What is the meaning of this? Of what good are these and thousands of other frightful accidents and incomprehensible sufferings which stagger men?

The arguments which are used to explain these phenomena explain nothing. These arguments always leave on one side the very essence of the question, and prove by this still more convincingly the impossibility of explaining these phenomena. I have fallen ill, because certain microbes have been carried to certain parts of my body; or the children were crushed before their mother's eyes, because damp acts in a certain manner upon iron; or Vierny was destroyed, because of the existence of certain geological laws! But the problem is to know exactly why these men and not others have been attacked by these horrible sufferings and how I may escape such occasions of suffering.

To this there is no reply. Reason on the contrary clearly shows me that there is not and that there cannot be a law according to which one man more than another should be exposed to these eventualities, that there are an immense number of accidents of this kind, and that, consequently, whatever I do, my life is exposed at every instant to all the innumerable chances of the most horrible sufferings.

If men who regard their life as individual existence, made only those deductions which follow inevitably from this manner of regarding life, they would not consent to live for a single instant. Not a single workman would live with a master who, in engaging him, reserved by contract the right, every time that he wishes to do so, to torture him by roasting him alive on a slow fire, by flaying him alive, by stretching him on the rack,—in a word, by perpetrating all the cruelties which he sees practised in his presence, without reason and without cause, on his workmen. If men really understood life as they say, not one would remain alive in the world, if only from fear of all the suffering so cruel and so entirely inexplicable which he sees around him and which may attack him at any moment.

Yet, though they know many easy ways of killing themselves, of going out of this life full of suffering, so cruel and so inexplicable, men live; they complain, they deplore their sufferings, but continue to live.

One cannot say that the cause of this is that joys are more numerous in this life than sufferings, first because simple reasoning, as well as philosophic researches into life, clearly show that all earthly life is a succession of sufferings, which are far from being compensated for by joys; on the other hand, we all know, of ourselves and from others, that men in such positions, for whom life is nothing but a succession of sufferings which increase until death without any possibility of being diminished, yet do not commit suicide, but cling to existence.

There is only one explanation of this strange contradiction; it is that all men know in the depth of their souls that all sufferings are always necessary, indispensable to the welfare of their life, and it is only for this reason that they continue to live, although they foresee them and are subjected to them. And if they revolt against suffering, it is only because with their false idea of life, which demands the welfare only of their individuality, all that is contrary to this welfare and does not lead to another visible welfare must seem something incomprehensible and therefore revolting.

Men fear sufferings and are astonished by them, as if they were something quite unexpected and incomprehensible. And yet every man is brought up by suffering; all his life is nothing but a succession of sufferings which he experiences himself and imposes on other beings; and it seems as if he ought to become used to suffering, not be afraid of it and not ask himself what is the cause of it. Every man who takes the trouble to think, will see that all pleasures are bought at the price of the sufferings of other beings; that all his sufferings are necessary to his pleasures; that without suffering there is no pleasure; that suffering and pleasure are two opposite states, each one called forth by the other and indispensable to each other. What then is the meaning of these questions which the reasonable man asks: "Wherefore? Why this suffering?"

Why does man, knowing that suffering and pleasure are united, ask "Why this suffering; to what purpose?" and not ask "Why this pleasure; to what purpose?"

The whole life of the animal, and of man in so far as he is animal, is nothing but an uninterrupted sequence of sufferings. The full activity of the animal, as well as that of man in so far as he is animal, is called forth only by suffering. Suffering is a painful sensation which calls forth activity, which drives away this painful sensation and thus evokes a condition of pleasure. The life of the animal, and that of man in so far as he is animal, instead of being disturbed by suffering owes its fulfilment to it. Consequently, sufferings give an impulse to life and therefore they ought to exist; what then does man mean when he asks "Why and to what purpose is suffering?"

The animal does not ask this question.

When the hungry perch torments the roach, when the spider torments the fly, and the wolf the sheep, they know they are doing what they ought to do, and that what happens ought to happen; consequently, when the perch, the spider, and the wolf are subjected to these tortures by other animals stronger than themselves, they, in fleeing, repelling, and freeing themselves, know that they are doing what they ought to do, and therefore they are fully convinced that what happens to them ought to happen. But a man entirely occupied in caring for his broken limbs on a field of battle, where he shattered the limbs of others; or he who is occupied only in trying to pass his term of solitary confinement in the best possible manner, after having himself directly or indirectly caused other persons to be imprisoned; or he who only seeks to beat off the wolves which tear him and to escape from them, after having himself slaughtered thousands of animals for food,—this man, I say, cannot accustom himself to the idea that all which happens to him ought to happen. He cannot admit it, because when he has been exposed to these sufferings he has not done what he ought to have done; and it seems to him that what happens ought not to happen. What more ought he then to do to save himself and to escape from the wolves which are tearing him?— that which is suitable to the nature of man as a reasonable being:—avow the sin which caused the suffering, repent of it and recognize the truth.

The animal suffers only in the present; therefore, the activity called forth by that suffering, directed to it in the present, fully satisfies it. But man suffers not only in the present, he suffers also in the past and in the future; consequently, if the activity called forth by suffering is only directed towards the present of the animal man, it cannot satisfy him. That activity alone which has for its aim the causes and the sequence of suffering in the past and in the future can satisfy the man who suffers.

An animal is locked up and breaks out of its cage;
it has an injured paw and licks the sore place; or it
is torn by another animal and tries to escape from it.
The law of its life is disturbed by an external cause,
and it employs its activity to re-establish it, and
what ought to happen, happens. But a man — I
myself or one of my neighbours—is in prison; or my
neighbour or I have a leg broken in battle; or I am
torn by wolves; the activity I employ for running
away from prison, for curing my leg, for escaping
from the wolves, does not satisfy me, because the
imprisonment, the injury to my leg, or the attacks
of the wolves constitute only a small part of my
suffering. I see the causes of my suffering in the
past, in my strayings from the way, and in those of
other men, and if my activity is not directed towards
the cause of the suffering, that is to say towards my
strayings, and if I do not make an effort to deliver
myself from it, I am not doing what I ought to do;
therefore the suffering appears to me to be something that ought not to be, and it assumes in reality
and in my imagination frightful proportions, which
exclude the possibility of life.

The cause of the suffering which the animal feels
is the transgression of the law of animal life; this
transgression manifests itself by the consciousness of
pain, and the activity called forth by that transgression is employed to remove the pain; to the
reasonable consciousness, the cause of the suffering
is the transgression of the law of life, of the reasonable consciousness; this transgression manifests
itself by the consciousness of the error of the sin,
and the activity called forth by this transgression of
the law tends to remove the error and the sin. And
just as the suffering of the animal calls forth an
activity applicable to the pain which takes away
its intensity, so the sufferings of the reasonable
being call forth an activity directed towards the

error, and this activity frees suffering of its painful character.

The questions :—" Why is it ?   To what purpose ? " which arise in the mind of man when he experiences suffering really or in imagination, show only that he has not recognized the activity which suffering ought to bring to life in him, activity which takes away from it its painful character.   And, indeed, the man who recognizes his life in animal existence is deprived of this activity which removes suffering ; and this so much the more the less widely he understands his life.

When a man who regards his life as individual existence discovers the causes of his individual suffering in his own error, when he discovers that he has fallen ill because he has eaten something unwholesome, when he has been beaten because he himself sought a quarrel, or when he is hungry and naked because he would not work ; when he recognizes that he suffers because he has done what he ought not to have done, and that in future he must act otherwise and direct his activity to the annihilation of his fault, then he will not revolt against suffering, he will bear it without grief, and often with joy. But when he has to bear suffering which goes beyond the limits in which he can perceive the link which unites the suffering to the fault, as when his suffering arises from causes always outside his individual activity, or when his suffering cannot have useful effects for himself or for another individuality, it seems to him that something is happening to him which ought not to happen, and he asks himself : Why is it ?   To what purpose ?   And not finding an object towards which he can direct his activity, he revolts against the suffering, which thus-becomes terrible torture.   But the greater part of the sufferings of man are precisely those of which the causes or the consequences (sometimes one sometimes the other) are hidden from his eyes in time and space : hereditary maladies, accidents, famines, railway accidents, fires, earthquakes, etc., which usually end in death.

The explanations which tend to show that this is necessary to give a lesson to our descendants, by showing them that they must not give way to passions which may influence posterity by transmitting diseases, that they must improve the state of the railroads, or be more prudent in the use of fire—all these explanations give me no satisfactory answer. I cannot recognize the meaning of my life in the spectacle of the errors of other men. My life and my longing for my own welfare absolutely belong to me, and are not a spectacle for other lives. Such explanations at the most furnish a subject for conversation, but they do not diminish the terror I feel in the presence of the absurdity of the sufferings which menace me and which make life impossible.

But even if it were possible to understand that, while making other men suffer by our faults, I by my sufferings bear the faults of others; even if we could understand, were it but vaguely, that all suffering indicates a fault which must be rectified by men in this life, there would still remain quite an enormous series of inexplicable sufferings.

A man alone in a forest is torn to pieces by wolves, a man is drowned, has perished by cold or by fire, or has simply fallen ill and died, and no one will ever know what he suffered; and there are thousands of such cases. To whom can this be of use?

In the eyes of the man who regards life as ar animal existence all this is inexplicable; because, for such a man, the link between suffering and fault is only in the phenomena visible to him, whilst in the sufferings which precede death this link completely escapes his intellectual perception.

For a man there are two possibilities. either not

recognizing the link between the sufferings experienced by him and his life, to continue to endure the greater part of his sufferings as tortures devoid of meaning ; or to recognize that my errors and the actions resulting from them [my sins, whatever they may be] are the cause of all. my sufferings without exception, and that these are the deliverance and redemption of my sins and of those of others.

Only these two relations to suffering are possible : according to the one, suffering is what it ought not to be because I do not see its external signification ; according to the other, suffering ought to come because I know its intrinsic importance for my true life. The first arises from considering as welfare the welfare of my individual life in particular ; the other arises from regarding as welfare the welfare of all my life past and future, linked indissolubly to the welfare of all men and all beings. According to the first of these points of view, suffering is inexplicable and cannot call forth any other activity than a despair and an irritation always increasing and which nothing can calm ; according to the second, suffering calls forth an activity which constitutes the movement of the true life, that is to say confession of sin, liberation from error, and submission to the law of reason.

In default of reason, the torture of suffering obliges man whether he will or no to recognize that his life does not lie in his individuality ; that his individuality is but the visible portion of his entire life ; that the external link between cause and effect which his individuality reveals does not coincide with the internal link between cause and effect which the reasonable consciousness always makes known to man.

The animal only sees the link uniting the fault and the suffering in conditions of time and space, whilst the man perceives it always in his consciousness outside of these conditions. Man recognizes always that the suffering, whatever it may be, is the consequence of his sin, whatever it may be, that the repentance of his sin alone delivers from suffering and brings welfare.

The whole life of man from the first days of his infancy consists only in coming to a knowledge of his sin by means of suffering and in liberating himself from his errors. I know that I entered into this life with a certain knowledge of thē truth, and that the farther I have wandered from it, the more my sufferings and those of other men have increased ; I know that the more I have liberated myself from error, the less suffering has there been for me and for others, and the greater has been the welfare which I have obtained. Consequently I know that the greater the knowledge of the truth that I shall carry away from this world, knowledge obtained even at the price of supreme suffering preceding death, the greater will be the welfare to which I shall attain.

The torments of suffering are experienced only by him who, having separated himself from the life of the world, not seeing those sins of his by which he brought sufferings into the world, considers himself innocent, and therefore rebels against those sufferings which he endures for the sins of the world.

And strange to say, this very thing which is manifest to the reason, mentally, is also confirmed by the one true activity of life, by love. Reason says that the man who recognizes the link uniting his sins and sufferings to those of the world, delivers himself from the torture of suffering ; love in reality confirms this.

Half of the life of every man passes in sufferings, which he not only does not recognize as torments, and does not notice, but even considers to be welfare ; and this proceeds solely from his bearing them as the consequences of errors and seeing in them a way of lightening the sufferings of beings whom he loves. So that the less he has of love, the more the man is exposed to the torments of suffering; whilst the greater the love is, the less the torment of suffering. But a life entirely rational, of which all the activity is manifested only in love, excludes the possibility of any suffering. The torment of suffering is nothing else than the pain felt by men when they try to break the chain of love for their ancestors, for their descendants, and for their contemporaries, which unites the human life to the life of the world.

CHAPTER XXXV

Physical sufferings constitute an indispensable condition of the life and welfare of men.

"And yet there is suffering, physical suffering. Why is there this suffering?" Men ask, "Why?" Because this is not only necessary for us, but because it is impossible to live without life being painful to us, might reply the One who has willed that we should suffer, He who has made pain as bearable as possible, He who as compensation has made the greatest possible welfare to flow from this "pain." Who does not know that the very first painful sensation is the first and chief means of preserving our body and of prolonging our animal life? Without this means of preservation we should all during infancy have burnt or mutilated our whole body for amusement. Physical pain preserves our animal individuality. Since pain serves to preserve the individuality, in the case of a child, it cannot be to a child the frightful torture that we know pain to be, when our reasonable consciousness is in its full

strength, when we resist pain and take it for something which ought not to be. With the animal and
the child pain is clearly defined and very slight,
never attaining to the degree of torment which it
reaches in a being endowed with reasonable consciousness. A child complains as much of the bite
of a flea as of an ailment which destroys his internal
organs. And the pain of a being void of reason
leaves no traces in his memory. Let us try to
remember the sufferings from pain of our childhood
and we shall see that not only can we not remember
them, but even that it is impossible to recall them
in imagination. The impression made on us by the
sight of the sufferings of children and animals is
rather our suffering than theirs. The outward
expression of suffering in unreasoning beings exceeds
by a great deal the pain itself, and calls forth in an
immeasurably greater degree our compassion than
the reality admits of. This is what we see in brain
diseases, delirium, typhus, and various forms of
agony.

At the period of life when the reasonable consciousness is still unawakened, and pain serves only
to preserve the individuality, pain is not tormenting;
but when the reasonable consciousness has become
accessible to man, pain is a means of influencing the
animal individuality to submit to reason; and in the
measure in which this consciousness awakens more
and more fully, pain becomes less and less tormenting.

In the main, it is only when we are in full possession of the reasonable consciousness that we are able
to speak of sufferings, because it is only from this
state that life commences, and those states of it which
we call sufferings. In this state the sensation of
pain can reach its greatest intensity or be reduced
to its lowest degrees. Indeed, everyone knows,
without having studied physiology, that sensibility
has its limits, and that once pain has reached a

certain limit either sensibility ceases and gives place to fainting, to insensibility, to fever,—or death occurs. The augmentation of pain then is a very clearly defined quantity, which cannot pass its limits. As for the painful feeling, it can increase indefinitely or be reduced to infinitesimal proportions, and this depends on our relation to it. Everyone knows how, by resigning himself to pain and by regarding it as a thing which ought to be, a man can cease to feel it and even experience joy in enduring it. Without speaking of martyrs, without speaking of Huss who sang at the stake, ordinary men, inspired only by the desire to prove their courage, bear without cries and without quailing operations regarded as most painful. There are limits to the increase of pain; as for the painful feeling this can be diminished indefinitely.

The anguish of pain is certainly terrible for men who have placed their life in the carnal existence. How should it not be terrible, when the power of reason which has been given to man to suppress the torment of suffering is directed only to augment it.

According to one of Plato's fables, God had assigned at the first a duration of seventy years to human life, but afterwards, perceiving that the condition of men became worse, He substituted the arrangement which now exists, that of leaving men ignorant of the hour of their death. To better show what is reasonable in the established arrangement we might make a fable that in the beginning men were created without the faculty of perceiving painful sensations, but afterwards for their welfare the present order was established.

If the gods had created men without the feeling of pain, they would very soon begin to ask for it; without the pains of childbirth women would give birth to children under such conditions that very few infants would live; without the faculty of feeling pain children and young people would destroy their bodies, grown men would never know the errors of other men of the past or present, nor, what is of most importance, their own errors—they would not know what they ought to do in this life, their activity would have no rational aim, they would never be able to reconcile themselves to the idea of carnal death, they could not possess love.

For the man who understands his life as the subjection of his individuality to the law of reason, pain not only is not an evil, but it is an indispensable condition of his animal life as well as of his rational life. If pain did not exist, the animal individuality would not be warned of the transgressions of its law; if the reasonable consciousness did not experience suffering, man would never know the truth and would be unaware of the law of his being.

But, the objector will say, you speak of your own individual sufferings; how can you deny those of others? Is not the sight of these sufferings the most acute suffering of all? men will say. But that is not their most secret thought. The suffering of others? But the sufferings of others, that is to say what you call sufferings, have always gone on and are going on. All men and all animals suffer and never cease to suffer. Is it possible that we have only heard of this to-day? Wounds, mutilations, hunger, cold, diseases, accidents of all sorts, and above all the birth-pains, without which none of us have come into the world, are not these all indispensable conditions of existence? You speak of the sufferings of others, but it is this, it is the lessening, the solacing of these sufferings, which forms the essence of rational life of men, to which the true activity of life is directed.

The one business of human life, is to understand the sufferings of individualities, the causes of human errors and the activity which it is necessary to exert to lessen them. If I am a man, an individuality, it is in order that I may understand the sufferings of other individualities; if I have a reasonable consciousness, it is in order that I may see in the sufferings of each separate individuality the common cause of suffering,—error,—and that I may destroy it in myself and in others.

How then can the material of his work be a suffering to the workman? It is as if the labourer said that an untilled field was a suffering to him. An untilled field can be a suffering only to him who wishes to see it tilled but does not regard the tilling of it as the task of his life.

The immediate action of love, which drives us to go to the aid of those who suffer and to destroy the common causes of suffering, that is to say error, is the one work which is given to man to accomplish, and which can procure for him this imprescriptible welfare which constitutes his life.

There is nothing but suffering for man, and it is this which obliges him whether he will or no to live that life which gives him his only welfare.

This suffering is the consciousness of the contradiction which exists between my state of sin and that of all the world, and not only the possibility, but the obligation of realising for myself, and not by the mediation of another, the whole truth in my life and in that of the world.

One cannot decrease this suffering either by participating in the sins of the world, or by shutting one's eyes to one's own sin, still less by ceasing to believe not only in the possibility but in the obligation (not for others but for myself), of realising the truth in my life and in the life of the world. By participating in the sin of the world, and by shutting my eyes to my own sin, I do but increase my suffering; by ceasing to believe in the possibility and the obligation of realising the truth in my life and in that of the world, I deprive myself of the strength to live.

This suffering is only softened by the consciousness and the activity of the true life, which put an end to the disproportion existing between the individual life and the end recognized by man. Whether he will or no, man must recognize that his life is not limited by his individuality existing from birth to death ; he must recognize that the goal of which he has a glimpse is accessible, and that the business of his life, which is inseparable from that of the whole world, is, has been, and will be always to advance towards that goal, by recognizing more and more his culpability, and by trying to realise more and more the truth in his life and in that of the world.   From the want of the reasonable consciousness, the suffering which results from error as to the meaning of his life drives the man whether he will or no towards the one true path of life, where there are neither obstacles nor evil, where there is but one welfare, always increasing, which nothing can disturb, which has never begun and can never end.

CONCLUSION

THE life of man is an aspiration towards welfare, and that to which he aspires is given to him.

Man only sees evil, under the form of death and sufferings, when he takes the law of his carnal and animal existence for that of his life.   Only when he, being a man, descends to the level of the beast— only then he sees death and suffering.   Death and suffering, like scarecrows, overwhelm him on all sides and drive him on to the only path that is open to him, the path of human life subjected to the law of reason and expressing itself in love.   Death and suffering are only the transgressions by man of the law of his life. For the man who lives according to its law there is neither death nor suffering.

"Come unto me, all ye that labour and are heavy laden, and I will give you rest. Take my yoke upon you, and learn of me, for I am meek and lowly in heart: and ye shall find rest unto your souls.

"For my yoke is easy and my burden is light" (Matt. xi. 28–30).

The life of man is an aspiration towards welfare; what he aspires to is given to him: a life which cannot be death, and a welfare that cannot be evil.

APPENDICES

---◆---

APPENDIX I

WE are accustomed to say: we will study life not
from the consciousness of our life, but in general
outside ourselves. But that amounts to saying
that we look at objects not with the eyes, but in
general outside ourselves.

We see objects outside of us, because we see
them by our eyes, and we only know the life outside
ourselves because we know it in ourselves. And we
see objects only as they appear to our eyes, and we
define the life outside us only as we know it in
ourselves. Now, we know the life in us as an
aspiration towards welfare. That is why, unless we
define life as an aspiration, it is impossible not only
to observe but even to see life.

The first and the principal action necessary in
order to arrive at the knowledge of living beings,
is to gather together in the conception of a single
living being a crowd of various objects, and to
separate that living being from all others. And
we only accomplish these two operations in virtue
of the same conception of life which we all have—
the conception of life as an aspiration towards my
own welfare, in so far as I am a being distinct from
all the rest of the world.

When we see a man on horseback, we know that

there is there neither a crowd of beings nor one single being, not because we observe all the parts of the man and of the horse, but because we see neither in the head, nor in the feet, nor in the other parts of the man and of the horse, such a distinct aspiration towards welfare, which we know in ourselves. And we only know that the man and the horse do not form one being, but two beings, because we recognize in them two distinct aspirations towards welfare, whilst in ourselves we know but one.

It is by that alone that we know that there is life in the association of the rider and horse, that there is life in a troop of horses, in birds, in insects, trees, grass. If we do not know that the horse desires welfare for himself, that the man also desires welfare for himself, that this also is the desire of every one of the horses in a troop, of every bird, of every lady-bird, of every tree, of every blade of grass, we do not see what distinguishes the beings, and for this reason we know nothing of the life; a regiment of cavalry, a troop of horses, the birds, the insects, the plants—all these would be as the waves of the sea, and the whole world would be to us netted together in a single uniform movement, in which it would be absolutely impossible to find life. If I know that the horse, the dog, the tick which fastens on the dog, are all living beings, and I can observe them, it is only because the horse, the dog, the tick have all their distinct aims, which to each one is his own welfare. I know this because I know myself as a similar aspiration towards welfare.

It is this aspiration towards welfare which is the basis of all knowledge of life; unless one grants that the aspiration towards welfare, that man feels in himself, is the very life and the distinctive sign of all life, it is impossible to study life, it is impossible to observe it. That is why observation begins when life is already known, and an observation which only bears upon the manifestations of life, can never (as the false science supposes) define life itself.

Men do not recognize the definition of life in the aspiration towards welfare which they find in their consciousness, but they grant the possibility of knowing this aspiration in the tick, and in virtue of this knowledge, supposititious and without foundation, of the welfare towards which the tick aspires, they make observations and draw deductions on the very essence of life.

All that I know of external life lies in the consciousness of my aspiration towards welfare. This is why it is only after I have come to know wherein consists my welfare and my life, that I shall be in the position to know in what consists the welfare and the life of other beings. But without knowing my own life it is absolutely impossible for me to know the welfare and the life of other beings.

Observations on other beings who strive for their own aims, which are unknown to me and which show a similarity to the welfare towards which I know that I strive,—these observations, I say, not only are incapable of facilitating my true knowledge of life, but they serve to hide it from me.

To study life in other beings, without having the definition of one's own, is the same thing as describing a circumference without knowing the centre. It is only after having taken as the centre an immutable point that one can describe a circumference. But whatever figures we draw, without a centre there cannot be a circumference.

APPENDIX II

FALSE science, which believes that in studying the phenomena which accompany life, it is studying life

itself, misrepresents by so doing the idea of life:
consequently the longer it studies the phenomena
which it calls life, the farther it goes away from the
idea of the life which it wishes to study.

They study first the mammals, then the vertebrate
animals, fish, plants, corals, cells, microscopical organisms, and they end by no longer knowing how to
distinguish that which lives from that which does
not, and by confounding organic with inorganic,
and one organism with another. This is carried
so far that what it is impossible to observe seems
to be the principal object of investigation and
observation.

It seems to them that the mystery of life and the
explanation of all is found in the comma-shaped
animalculæ, supposititious rather than visible, to-day
discovered, to-morrow forgotten. They suppose that
the explanation of everything lies in those beings
which are contained in microscopical beings, and in
those which are contained in these again, and so on
ad infinitum, as if the infinite divisibility of the little
were not an infinity just as much as the infinity of
the large. The mystery will only be revealed when
the infinity of the little shall have been investigated
to the end, that is to say, never. And men do not
see that by imagining that the solution of the
question is to be found in the infinitely small, they
prove in an indubitable manner that the question
has been wrongly put. And this last degree of
insanity, which shows clearly all the absurdity of
the investigations, this degree, I say, is regarded as
the triumph of science; the supreme degree of
blindness appears to be the acme of penetration.
These men are wandering in a blind alley, and have
clearly proved to themselves the falsity of that way
along which they have been going, and yet their
enthusiasm is without bounds: "Let us only make
our microscopes a little stronger, and we shall appre-

hend the transition of the inorganic into the organic, of the organic into the psychic, and all the mystery of life will be revealed to us."

In studying shadows instead of objects, men have completely forgotten that object the shadow of which they were studying, and by plunging deeper and deeper into the shadow, they have reached total darkness, and rejoice that the shadow is dense.

In the consciousness of man, life signifies the aspiration towards welfare. The chief end and the task of life of all humanity, is to explain in what this welfare consists and to give a more and more exact definition of it.

But because this task is difficult, because it is not a mere bagatelle, but a serious work, men decide that the definition of this welfare cannot be found there where it lies, that is to say in the reasonable consciousness of man, and that consequently it must be looked for everywhere save there where it is indicated.

This resembles the conduct of a man to whom exact instructions have been given in writing as to what he needs ; and who, not knowing how to read it, should throw away the paper containing these instructions and ask of all who pass by if they do not know what he needs.

Men seek everywhere except in the consciousness of man itself for the definition of life, that is to say the aspiration towards welfare, which is written in ineffaceable characters in the human soul.

It is the more strange as the whole of humanity, in the persons of its wisest representatives, beginning with the Greek maxim : " Know thyself," have always said, and continue to say, quite the contrary. All the religious doctrines are nothing else than definitions of life, aspirations towards real, undeceptive welfare accessible to man

APPENDIX III

THE voice of reason makes itself heard in man more and more clearly; man more and more often tries to listen to this voice; and the time is coming, and has already come, when this voice has become stronger than that which leads men towards individual welfare and delusive duty. It becomes more and more evident, on the one hand, that the life of individuality with its seductions cannot give welfare; on the other hand, that the payment of every debt, prescribed by men, is only a deceit which takes from man the possibility of paying his sole debt—to that rational and good principle from which he emanates. That ancient deceit which demands belief in that which has no rational explanation is already worn out, and it is impossible to return to it.

Men used to say, " Do not reason, but believe in that duty which we prescribe. Reason will deceive you. It is faith alone which will reveal to you the true good of life." And man tried to believe this, and did believe it, but intercourse with other men showed him that they believe in something quite different and affirm that their belief yields much greater good. It became imperative that man should solve the question which of the many beliefs is nearest to the truth ; and only reason can decide this.

And man always cognises everything through reason, and not through faith. It was possible to deceive him, affirming that he cognises through faith and not through reason ; but as soon as he knows two faiths and sees men professing an alien faith in the same way in which he himself professes his own, he is inevitably forced to decide this matter by his reason. A Buddhist, who has learned to know Mahommedanism, if he still remains a Buddhist does so not through faith but through reason. As soon as he is confronted with another faith and by the question, which will he reject, his own or the one offered to him ? the question is inevitably solved by reason. And if after having become acquainted with Mahommedanism he remains a Buddhist, the previous blind faith in Buddha is already inevitably based on rational grounds.

The attempts made in our time to infuse man with spirituality through faith alone, ignoring reason—are like attempts to feed a man without using his natural means.

Mutual intercourse has shown to men that basis of cognition common to all of them, and men can no longer return to their fallacies ; and the time is coming and has come already, when the dead will hear the voice of the Son of God, and having heard will revive.

It is impossible to stifle this voice, for it is the voice not of some single being, but of the whole rational consciousness of humanity, which makes itself heard in every separate man as well as in the best men of humanity; and now already in the majority of men.

MR. H. W. MASSINGHAM ON "LIFE"

EVERY now and again there arise in the world teachers who set aside the questions which men usually ask themselves or each other and are occupied solely with one problem—the meaning of life. Nothing else seems to them to be so important, and in the end, whether during their life or after it, society begins after its fashion to agree with them. These men do not belong purely to the type that we call philosophers. They not only observe life clearly, but they are so impressed with its seriousness that they find it impossible to govern their own existence on lines that are not in harmony with the truth that they have discovered about it. They can no longer share the average thoughts of their time. They must either change the main current of those thoughts or they must themselves withdraw from it. The stronger remain and aim at leading their fellows with them to the high tableland to which they themselves have painfully climbed. Among this latter type of human spirits few rarer or greater have appeared than Count Lyof Tolstoy.

Nothing is more impressive about this remarkable man than the complete unity of his life and his intellectual work. . . . Through the complexity of modern organisation Count Tolstoy has followed a single clue which runs equally through his artistic and his philosophical writings. This man, whose power lies so especially in the emotional presentation of life, has for more than twenty years never written without a definite moral aim. And what he has preached he has practised. He has seen events in their conventionally dramatic aspects—in war, in society, in European capitals, and

on the country estates of a rich nobleman—and he
has come to prefer the lot of a peasant and to find
his happiness in ministering to the needs of the
hungry and helpless. . . . But his outlook upon a
world grown complex beyond the imagination of
simpler forms of society is singularly broad.   He
has surveyed the entire sphere of our modern
activities, faith, philosophy, the theory and practice
of art, and, above all, the social and political fabric.
This double service of personal affection and consistent
teaching stands at once for and against the world—
for a conception of its true life and against its
accepted interpretation of life.   It is impossible not
to listen to him, for he speaks with unexampled
clearness and simplicity   And for many of us, too,
it seems as if this man in the peasant's dress, who
scatters his thoughts freely for those who want them,
and preaches to a world governed by force the
simple doctrine of persuasive reason, has in the
main laid down or revived the lines on which must
proceed the moral and intellectual battle of our day
and of the days that are to come.
     What is the secret of this attraction?   First of
all, it is, as I have said, that Tolstoy has lived the
life, and that his work in fiction and criticism traces,
step by step, the road of his own pilgrim's progress ;
and, secondly, that he associates himself with an
eternally interesting topic.   His Pierre; his Levin,
his Nekhludoff, pass before our eyes chiefly that we
may see through them the passage of Tolstoy's own
soul, and of all human souls, from death to life. . . .
Nowhere, however, has Tolstoy applied himself to
the task of elucidating what he regards as the one
important stage in individual existence more
thoroughly than in the philosophical work known as
Life, a book . . . of especial value as a key to
Tolstoy's method and belief, . . . and singularly
complete in itself.   It does not examine the practical
consequences of its doctrine, as to which Tolstoy's

life and his more directly didactic writings furnish
a finished and consistent key. It is concerned
purely with what Mr. Morley has called "the bright
dawn of life in the soul," and in its arrangement is
a continuous treatise on human nature, without
regard either to religious dogma or to earlier
philosophical conceptions. In a word, it is a
thoroughly original and powerful work of self-
examination, with consequences that seem to me to
be of the deepest importance to the life of our times.

Tolstoy introduces his subject with an illustration
drawn from the life of a miller who, . . . instead of
concentrating all his thought and effort on the kind
of flour which he is grinding, devotes it entirely to
the study of the river. There, he thinks, lies the
true secret of the mill. The miller's mistake comes
from the materialist idea of examining non-
conscious or remote phenomena and their supposed
causes as a key to the mystery of human nature.
That key, says Tolstoy, is to be found only in the
application of the old Greek saying, "Know
thyself." . . . Man knows himself first as a rational
being ruling the animal; secondly, as an animal
governed by what Tolstoy calls "rational consciousness"; and, thirdly, as matter governed by the
animal. The materialist view is therefore doomed
to sterility on account both of its unpractical method
and of its ignorance of the character of the problem
with which it has to deal. A man must cease gazing
down at the bewildering flow of the river of physical
life, and get back to his business.

Orthodox science, however, is not, in Tolstoy's
view, the only force in modern intellectual life
which has set the mind of man on the wrong track.
Just such another offender is the Church—the
"Pharisees" who unite with the "Scribes" in a
pessimistic and unpractical conclusion about life.
Life, says science, is to be explained by the
examination of physical laws which in man's own

body are performed unconsciously and independently of him—and therefore cannot be fully known—and which, in external matter, cannot even be understood by him.   Life, says the Church, consists in preparing, by means of the Sacraments or through Faith, for a future existence, which, in contrast with the life of labour and suffering, of which alone we have any idea, shall be, in Tolstoy's ironic description of it, "immortal, innocent, and idle."   Both these views abandon the sensible meliorist condition which Tolstoy adopts—namely, that man can act for his own well-being, that he can act here and now, and that his enlightened reason, his "rational consciousness," fully reveals to him the law of life of which he stands in need. . . .

First of all, what is life? Science can give no answer to this question.   It seeks to explore the laws and relations of force without defining what force is.   Furthermore, in observing the struggle for life which goes on in animals, it declares that that struggle is the source of life itself and its real business, thus placing itself in easy agreement with the coarse herd—the practical Nietzsches of the world who act on this principle.   Finally, science, studying a higher kind of being only through the laws affecting lower beings, can never instruct a man as to how he is to act—i.e., can never constitute a safe guide to "conduct."   It does not, for example, tell a man what he is to do with the piece of bread in his hand, whether he is to eat it himself, or to give away to another, or, if so, to whom he is to give it.   On the other hand, all mankind, save its lowest types, have long had as their common patrimony that great body of religious teaching which, whether it is Indian or Chinese or Christian in origin, unites in regarding life not-as the pursuit of individual happiness but as the sacrifice of self. All these religions are penetrated by the conviction of the irrationality of the purely individual life, whether this is lived for one's self or whether the circle of individual pursuit is enlarged so as to include one's family or one's country—or one's Empire. The faculty of reason, working through man's greatest teachers, whom he reverences even when he does not follow them, thus informs the individual that personal happiness cannot exist for him. So that the first operation of reason on man is to poison his existence—to bring him face to face with a terrible contradiction and leave him a prey to it. . . . At this stage of experience life seems to come to a dead stop, but, adds Tolstoy, it only seems to stop; really it has just begun.

What, now, is the second function of rational consciousness after it has expounded to man the futility of his animal life? In the reasoning which follows there is much to remind the reader of Arnold's *Literature and Dogma*, to which it is clear that Tolstoy is in some measure indebted. Arnold, however, with all his seriousness and insight, does not possess Tolstoy's constant faith, his deep affectionateness, and his broad and noble optimism, and therefore the writings of the earlier religious thinker, while they have the persuasiveness which belongs to his successor, lack the moral elevation which gives to *Life* the character of a great poem of humanity.

The "call," says Tolstoy, is to a new and high activity of reason, in obedience to the essential law of man's life. Just as the animal discovers that it will not do for it simply to obey the more elementary laws of its being, namely, to lie still and breathe, but that it must follow the higher law of seeking for food and reproducing its species, so rational consciousness arouses man to search for the path of his true well-being. This is not an accidental but an inevitable process. The spiritual birth, like the natural birth, occurs because the tabernacle of the old life is destroyed. . . .

Mysterious, however, as is this new birth, and mortally depressing are its first painful experiences, there is nothing about them to dismay the mind of man.   He has got to the point which Schopenhauer describes, of surveying his animal life and disapproving it.   But, as Tolstoy insists, his new life is progress in an entirely new direction to the old.   It is progress upwards.   His wings have carried him, without his knowing, to a height from which he looks down on the abyss and is terrified at it.   But he forgets that if he had not wings he could not have raised himself at all to this altitude of contemplation.   His true course, therefore, is not to look down but to trust to his wings, and go freely whither they carry him.   One thought in particular should give him confidence.   The difference between him and the animals is at once shown.   An animal ceasing to work for its individual welfare ceases to live.   On the contrary, life—and a life essentially healthy and natural to him—opens itself out to the man who has taken this course.   Moreover, he cannot go back. . . .

Yet another consideration drives man inevitably along the road of his new life.   The condition of his individual well-being is that all other men should love him and serve him more than they love and serve themselves.   But every man has this idea about his own personality.   Therefore happiness can only be realised when all creatures live for the good of others.   The strife among the pleasure-seekers turns the world into a vast battlefield, though convention hides from us the intensity and cruelty of the struggle.   On the other hand, the past history of man shows him that the true movement of life consists in the diminution of this war between individuals and in an approach to human brotherhood and unity. . . .

Rational consciousness has thus led man, by one road or another, to the discovery that the one reasonable activity of mankind is Love, which rids him at once of the fears that beset his animal existence and of his old absorbing, but essentially morbid, interest in the end of that existence. What is the natural manifestation of this activity? Tolstoy insists on some essential qualities. Love must be universal and complete. It must extend to all men, and it must amount to nothing less than the surrender of self. Therefore it must be a present and not a future love. . . .

Love, in a word, is not the preference of some people to others. It is the preference of all others to one's self. It is a state of goodwill (*bienveillance*) to all the world — a state which is common to children, who are fond of everybody, and who do not, until later on in their lives, learn to discriminate and calculate between one kind of affection and another. . . .

The latter chapters of this remarkable work concern themselves with a metaphysical analysis of death. "What is death?" asks Tolstoy, as he has previously asked the corresponding question, "What is life?" He answers that there is no death, and adds that this answer is not a mere sophistry, but a necessary deduction from the facts of consciousness. . . .

The fear of death arises from the old contradiction between the two opposing views of life. A man feels that he ought to have real life, and does not have it. That this is his actual feeling is shown by the action of suicides, who rush to death because they fear false life. Emptiness and darkness are men's postulates about death, but they fix their eyes on this blank because real life is not apparent to them.

The natural man, however, still has his reply ready to these arguments. He has lived so many years now, fifty, sixty, seventy—this term he sees is coming to an end. "Not at all," replies Tolstoy, in the chapter which I now summarise, " your *Ego*—your real self—is not a body which has gone on with its mechanical work for so many years. It is a-something which thinks and feels, always differently. ' You ' are not the ' you ' of twenty or ten years ago. Not only is your body changed in every particle from what it was, but even your consciousness has been suspended—as every day by sleep. It has also been divided into successive and well-marked stages of consciousness, such as boyhood and youth. . . .

" And this life of yours is an unending movement, involving continual changes in your relationship to the world—*i.e.*, in the degree of love which you entertain for it. Stop that movement and death indeed presents itself robed in all its terrors. Go on loving and loving more and you mix more and more with the eternal movement of life." . . .

It is to the attempt to realise this " Christianity of feeling and action " that Count Tolstoy's life and his intellectual and artistic work are devoted—an effort which has brought him, like his Master, into conflict with every established authority in the modern world. When will his conception of the advent of the enlightened man—whom he continually calls the Son of God—be realised in the history of humanity? We cannot tell. Certain it is that such a witness to it cannot be denied. It is there—at once accusing and comforting. For with Tolstoy, and men like Tolstoy, light comes into the world, and we feel that in its sacred radiance the common life of man is transfigured and absorbed.

[Abbreviated from an article by Mr. H. W. Massingham, " The Philosophy of a Saint," in *The Contemporary Review*, December 1900, by kind permission of Mr. Massingham.]

Smiths', Typ., Hutton Street, E.C., and Fleet Works, St Albans.

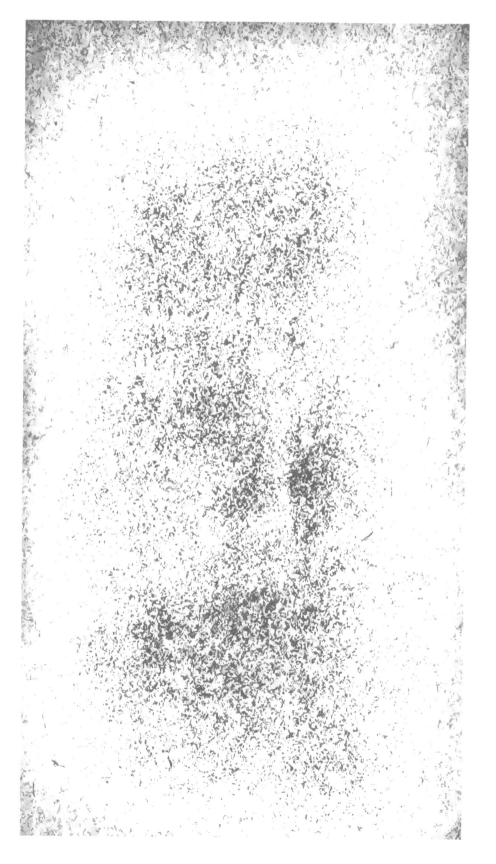

14 DAY USE

RETURN TO DESK FROM WHICH BORROWED

LOAN DEPT.

This book is due on the last date stamped below, or
on the date to which renewed.
Renewed books are subject to immediate recall.

6 Jan '59 J PZ	REC'D LD
	MAY 22 1961
REC'D LD	
DEC 18 1958	
11 Ja'59 I Z	
REC'D LD	
JAN 6 1959	
9 May'60 RT *HURST*	
JUN 9 1960	
REC'D LD	
MAY 17 1960	
23 May61 BM	

General Library
University of California
Berkeley

ImTheStory.com

Personalized Classic Books in many genre's

Unique gift for kids, partners, friends, colleagues

Customize:

- Character Names
- Upload your own front/back cover images (optional)
- Inscribe a personal message/dedication on the
  inside page (optional)

Customize many titles Including
- Alice in Wonderland
- Romeo and Juliet
- The Wizard of Oz
- A Christmas Carol
- Dracula
- Dr. Jekyll & Mr. Hyde
- And more...